W9-BMQ-054

ACT NOW!

How I Turn
Ideas into
MILLION-DOLLAR
Products

ACT
NOW!

Kevin Harrington
King of the Infomercial
with **William L. Simon**

Health Communications, Inc.
Deerfield Beach, Florida

www.hcibooks.com

Several quotes have been used in Chapters 5, 6, and 7, from a case study on Kevin Harrington's company and career prepared by Neil Churchill, professor of business at Southern Methodist University and later at Harvard. Wendy Wolf assisted in the preparation. The case study is copyright ©1991 by Neil C. Churchill and is used by permission.

Library of Congress Cataloging-in-Publication Data

Harrington, Kevin.
    Act now! : turning your idea into the next million-dollar product / Kevin Harrington with William L. Simon.
        p. cm.
    Includes index.
    ISBN-13: 978-0-7573-0756-0 (trade paper)
    ISBN-10: 0-7573-0756-6 (trade paper)
    1. Harrington, Kevin. 2. Infomercials — United States.
3. New products — United States — Marketing. 4. Businessmen — United States — Biography. I. Simon, William L. II. Title.
HF6146.T42H3367 2009
659.14'3 — dc22

                                                          2009002912

HCI, its logos, and marks are trademarks of Health Communications, Inc.

Publisher: Health Communications, Inc.
        3201 S.W. 15th Street
        Deerfield Beach, FL 33442-8190

Cover design by Larissa Hise Henoch
Interior design and formatting by Dawn Von Strolley Grove

For Crystal, Tim,
and my parents, Charles and Mary Harrington
—KH

And for
Arynne, Victoria, David,
Sheldon, Vincent, and Elena
—WLS

CONTENTS

Part Three: Advice from the Trenches

Whatever you vividly imagine,
ardently desire,
sincerely believe,
and enthusiastically act upon
must inevitably come to pass.

—Paul Meyer, businessman and author

INTRODUCTION

Some people take life as it comes; some grab it by the ears and shake and shake.

For better or worse, I'm one of the shakers, which is the reason the path I've followed has been so full of surprises and has, in some small ways, changed the world we live in. The infomercial has become a mega-billion-dollar business, it has become a social institution, and it has unexpectedly become an intriguing route that makes it possible for anyone with a little drive and determination to become wealthy beyond his or her dreams, as I show in Parts Two and Three of this book.

It always amuses me when I hear people deride the infomercial as if it were a tool for parting the undereducated on the lower side of the earning's curve from their money. One of the world's most powerful selling tools, the infomercial is the least recognized for its impact and selling power. Americans alone spend millions of dollars each month buying from direct-response ads on television, and the United States is now only a small part of the global market.

The story I tell here is partly about my own role in bringing all this together, and the many celebrities I have met along the way. But even more, the story reveals the incredible path to riches that so many people have already followed—people like Arnold Morris, the incredible pitchman I discovered selling Ginsu knives to crowds of twenty or thirty people; I put him on television where he sold the knife sets to hundreds of millions of people. And it is about the parade of innovators, inventors, and creators who every year suddenly find themselves earning millions through an infomercial or through the online shopping channels.

You, too, can become one of them . . . if you Act Now! Good luck!

PART ONE

GEARING UP

1

NEVER TOO YOUNG

*A man who gives his children habits
of industry provides for them better than
by giving them a fortune.*

—Richard Whately

From my father, Charlie Harrington, I gained a love of being
in business and the entrepreneurial pleasure of being my
own boss. I'd like to think I also inherited his great Irish/
German innkeeper's talent for making every stranger feel like
an old friend.

From my mother, Mary, I gained a respect for the idea of
earning money and a devotion to the Catholic religion; the first
has lasted all my life so far; the second lasted only through high
school.

My father grew up in Cincinnati, enlisted in the Army Air
Corps early in World War II, and became a decorated hero pilot-
ing P-40 fighter-bombers over Germany. He would go out on a

mission with ten or fifteen other aircraft, and only six or eight of them would make it home. But when my dad had completed the required 25 missions, he and a bunch of his buddies turned down a transfer back to the States and kept flying. He eventually flew some 138 combat missions, was shot down twice, and collected a bunch of medals. That passion for doing a job well survived through everything he would do in life. I loved having a war hero for a father, and I loved listening to his stories.

On his way home from combat, he told his closest pilot buddy, wingman Thomas Sutton, "There's only one guy in the world I trust like my brother, and that's you. You're going to marry my sister." I grew up knowing that man as my Uncle Sut.

When I was born in 1956, my parents and three older siblings (there would eventually be six children in the family) were already settled in the upscale Hyde Park section of Cincinnati, a neighborhood that my mother, the daughter of a bank president, had insisted on. The decision became one of the root causes of too many heated conversations in the Harrington household—my mother always busting my father about the need for more money. But those conversations had one virtue: they helped shape one of the cornerstone values behind my drive for success.

My father became a restauranteur, an entrepreneurial wildcat who over the years owned a string of pubs, nightclubs, supper clubs, bars—more than a dozen places. For a time he had a club he called Harrington's Bar and Grill, and he started the Mt. Lookout Tavern that is still a landmark in Cincinnati. One of his greatest claims to fame was the Bachelor's Club, a fancy steak and lobster restaurant that, after closing its doors at 2:30 AM on Saturdays, turned into an after-hours joint, a gathering place for cops and singers, nightclub pianists, showgirls, the cast of any play or musical passing through town—the entertainment elite of Cincinnati. Everybody knew my father as "Charlie," the glad-handing barkeep people loved to clap on the back and exchange jokes and insults with.

I had tremendous respect for my father, who had been a boxer in college and was a tough-guy type everybody knew not to mess with—he kept a baseball bat under the bar at whatever restaurant he was running, and there wasn't any doubt he'd use it if he needed to. But he worked unbelievably long hours, six days a week from noon until at least 2:00 AM, so in the early years I rarely saw him. My father's long hours inspired my own. In the summers from age nine, I started mowing people's lawns and lugging back their trash cans from the curb. One lawn job was a mile away; I pushed the mower there and back and would make $1.50 for two or three hours of work. Another job I took was selling newspapers after school on street corners at Mt. Lookout Square. While other kids were playing, I was always hustling, doing something to make a buck. By the time I was ten, I'd saved $500—probably the equivalent of a few thousand dollars today.

The years of not seeing my father changed when I was eleven. I went to him one day and said, "I'd like to have a job with you at the Bachelor's Club," his restaurant at the time. This simple request marked the beginning of my learning the ethic of hard work. I'd come home from school, do my homework, jump on a bus, transfer twice to reach the restaurant, and work till 11:00 PM. On Saturdays, I would come in at 11:00 AM to clean up from the night before and continue working until 2:30 the next morning, when I'd take a break to enjoy the breakfast buffet dad laid out for the entertainers who would be dropping in. After that I'd clean up, usually finishing around 5:00 in the morning and finally making it home around 8:00—almost a 24-hour workday.

My father worked me hard. If he was prince of the palace, I was the equivalent of the lowliest stable boy—busing tables, scraping dishes, and putting everything through the noisy, steamy dishwasher. Working for my father gave me a better sense of what the outer reaches of hell might be like than the vision given to me by the nuns where I went to school. But I wore another hat as well, doing the duties of what major restaurants call *garde-manger*: prepping salads, steaks, lobsters, and anything else that needed to be made ready for the oven or grill. I worked forty hours a week at a salary of only $1 an hour, when the national minimum wage was $1.40. My father said, "I don't know if you're going to work as hard as the rest of the crew." I ran circles around everyone else. It only took two months before my father started paying me the full $1.40. But that 40 percent raise only added $16 to my salary—before taxes.

The chef's wife called one day to say, "Butch can't come in tonight. He's been in a terrible accident. He's in really bad shape." "That's terrible," my father said. "I'm so sorry to hear it. How long will he be out?" She replied, "Oh, he'll be in tomorrow." It was my first introduction to how some people allow a little talent to go to their heads. Dad would have to cook, and I'd take over as assistant chef—at age eleven or twelve. When he'd have to go out front to solve a problem, I'd be left to do the cooking.

Another time, Dad showed up at his restaurant of the moment and noticed an extra cash register on the bar: the bartender was putting some of the money in the restaurant's register, and some of it in the other one, which he expected to slip out of the door with at the end of his shift when no one was looking. Then there was the afternoon when my father noticed that a delivery driver was wheeling in two kegs of beer and going back out with two empties. My dad stopped the driver before he could pull away. He called to me, "Come over here, son. Put your hand on this keg"—one of the empties the driver had just loaded. "What do you feel?" my dad asked.

"It's cold," I said.

"What does that tell you?"

"I guess it's not really empty."

The driver had been bringing in two full kegs, and then wheeling one empty and one full one back onto the truck. My dad's lesson was, "Don't trust anybody." Maybe that was true in the restaurant business, where he had to assume everyone in the place was stealing from him. Yet somehow I ended up with the opposite attitude—trusting everyone until they give me reason not to.

But I did learn the unhappy lesson that a lot of people are

flakes, and a lot of the rest simply can't be counted on. And I learned that in a small business, you have to work the business yourself to make sure you aren't being cheated.

Four years of slaving for my father equipped me with a solid knowledge of restaurant economics and enough kitchen skills to hold down a job as an assistant chef, if I wanted one. I was aiming higher though, with a pair of push-pull forces working on my psyche. The push came from friends of my dad who were always telling me, "You've got to be like your father." It also came from my dad himself, who was forever lighting a fire under me: "You've got to find something you really want to go out and do on your own." His influence outweighed the opposite messages from my mother: "Why would you want to have your own business—look at your father!" Meaning: *Look how hard he works and how tight the money always is for this family.*

The pull force came from guys in my neighborhood. It's what often happens, I guess, for kids whose friends come from much richer families. The father of one kid I hung out with owned the Cincinnati Reds baseball team. One of my best buddies, Mark, was the son of the chairman and CEO of Kroger, the national grocery chain. I'd sometimes be invited on vacations with them to tag along as a companion for Mark, and we'd fly off to Palm Beach or wherever on his dad's private jet.

I had the bug. I wanted to have a business of my own, and I wanted to make *real* money.

One day another friend, not one of the rich ones, started telling me about a man his parents knew who was selling a product called Brewer Cote, a driveway sealant. Everybody who comes from a part of the country where the winters are long and bitter knows how pathetic an asphalt driveway can look when spring finally comes. My friend thought repaving driveways was a business the two of us could get into together. He was sixteen and already had his driver's license, and he had spotted me as a go-getter.

We went and talked to the distributor, who told us, "Guys pull in here and load up a fifty-five-gallon drum of this sealant, and they're making a fortune." He said, "Why don't you guys give it a try?"

The division of labor was a no-brainer. I was going to knock on doors and do the selling; my buddy was going to load up the product, bring it to the work sites, and do the labor. We chipped in and bought a truck for $150.

I had picked up a little of that Irish gift of gab from hearing my father entertain his restaurant and bar patrons. The idea of knocking on doors and finding buyers for our new service didn't faze me a bit. Still, it wasn't exactly as easy as I had imagined. Just picture the scene: you're sitting at home after dinner, reading the newspaper or watching television, and there's a knock at the door. You answer the knock and stand there listening to a sales pitch for having your driveway beautifully restored to like-new condition, at a very reasonable price.

Except that the salesman giving you this pitch is a fresh-faced kid of fifteen who, when you ask, tells you in all candor that he and his partner represent the entire workforce offering you this deal.

I was part Irish: the gift of language was, for me as for my forebears, a tool to win one's goal. After I had heard "no" a few too many times, a change of tactics was obviously called for. But what?

The next man who answered my knock heard a new line: "We want to reseal your driveway to get rid of the cracks so next winter when it freezes, your paving won't keep getting broken up even worse. You probably think we're too young to trust with the job, so here's what we want to do. Let us do your driveway for just the cost of materials, $25. If you don't like the work, you don't have to pay for it. But if you're happy with the work, I want you to let me put up a sign at your sidewalk and let me show neighbors before and after pictures of your driveway."

The third householder I pitched that way agreed to the deal. We were in business. From then on, in each new neighborhood, I'd find a householder who'd let these two kids do his driveway for the cost of materials and then show the photos to his neighbors. It worked like a charm. I was selling three or four resurfacing jobs on every block. On a good day, we would do five or six driveways, and since this was during the summer, we could work six days a week, clearing about $50 to $80 after the cost of materials from each job. As the business quickly grew, we hired other youngsters to do the grunt work. There were weeks when we made $2,000 to $3,000 sealing driveways. To fill in over the winters, I found a job selling Babee Tenda safety high chairs; I put boxes up at the shopping malls that said "Mother-to-be?

Win a Free Gift!" I'd go visit the ladies who filled out the little form, bringing her the free gift, and then explain the benefits of the safety high chair. Most of the time, it was an easy sale.

I attended Purcell, an all-boys Catholic high school, where I was in a special program that offered college credit for high school courses. Math was my favorite subject, and I did very well in it, but much less well in English. I don't know if there's any correlation to that in terms of my business success, but sometimes I wonder.

Sports were important to me. In junior high, I had been a halfback and captain of the football team. I was also the smallest guy on the team, weighing in at just ninety-eight pounds. In high school, I was up against three-hundred-pound guys, and my father insisted on my finding a different sport. I switched to wrestling, becoming one of the top wrestlers in the state. Through four years of varsity wrestling, I gained discipline. The grueling daily practices began with running up and down four flights of stairs one hundred times.

When I turned sixteen, I bought my own car, a brand-new 1972 MG. Until then, I had been borrowing my parents' car but, at barely five feet tall, I had to sit on a pillow to see over the steering wheel. That cool sports car was built to my size: no pillow needed. Plenty of my friends from wealthy families had cars, but they were all bought for them by Daddy. Driving out of the showroom with a car I bought from my own earnings was a very proud moment in my life. But there was more to it than simply patting myself on the back. It was as if the skies had opened. If I could buy a car at age sixteen with my own money, it seemed like a promise that I could achieve almost anything I set my mind to. What a sense of exhilaration and empowerment!

What's more, that car led me into my next career move.

LEAPING AHEAD

In those days, thirty-five years ago, car makers didn't put rust-proofing on the underside of the chassis. I've always figured it was a conscious decision, a tactic of designed obsolescence. Every winter storm would bring out the city trucks spreading salt to melt the snow and ice. That salt, sloshed up onto the chassis of every car from beneath, would do a very effective job eating away at the metal, leaving many cars with gaping holes in their fenders.

A man phoned me one night shortly after I had bought my MG and offered to rustproof my car. He said the price was only $119, and the work would be guaranteed for the life of the car. As protection for my new hot sports car, that sounded like a bargain. I told him to come see me.

When he showed up the next afternoon at my parents' home, he introduced himself and said, "Where's your dad? I want to talk to him about his new car."

I explained that the person he had talked to on the phone was me and that I was the owner of the car. He wanted to know, "How does a kid like you get a car like this?"

"I'm a salesman," I told him. I could see the gears turning in his head: *This boy must be a damned good salesman if he could earn the money to buy an MG at his age.*

He asked me to come in and meet the owners of his company. They were based in Columbus, just beginning to build up their business in Cincinnati, and they offered me a job selling on commission. By that time I had gotten pretty fed up with the driveway-sealing business, because we were out of work for the whole winter, until the ice and snow melted, and selling high chairs to pregnant ladies wasn't really what a high school kid wanted to be doing. I was glad for the opportunity to dive into something new with a year-round opportunity.

I know this will sound mighty strange, but in those days the Cincinnati newspaper published a listing of the folks who had just bought a new car—name, address, and the car's make and model. Most of the people I called were happy to let me come and talk to them.

My little dog-and-pony show included a set of pictures of rusted-out cars, but I hardly needed them. The rustproofing made good sense. I'd tell the car owner, "That automobile is your second most expensive purchase. You can protect it for only $119."

I had been honing my skills at handling objections. From the get-go, I was closing about 80 percent, making ten to fifteen sales a week, sometimes taking home only $500 in a week, other times as much as $1,500. While kids from my school were scooping ice cream or flipping burgers for $1.60 an hour, I was earning twice as much as the next best salesmen for my company—and he was working to support a family.

As the company expanded and prospered, they began hiring new salesmen at a lower commission rate than I was making, extracting a promise from me not to tell anyone how much more I was getting. But I guess it finally began to gnaw at the owners that they were paying me so much. I was making a lot of money, of course, but making a lot for the company in the process. They lost sight of that and announced they were cutting my commission rate from 20 percent to 10 percent.

I said good-bye.

And now ... ?

I was sixteen years old, but looked more like fourteen—my growth spurt wouldn't start until I was a senior in high school. My summer earnings had been running around $2,000 to $4,000 a month, as much as many experienced factory workers, even as much as a lot of computer programmers with college degrees. But I was already setting my goals higher.

If I could make that kind of money selling hundred-dollar rustproofing, how much could I make if I were selling some big-ticket item? I began to scour the "salesman wanted" ads in the newspaper and paying visits to some of the more likely-sounding companies. It's fascinating how quickly you can tell if an operation is too sleazy to take seriously. When the guy doing the interviewing was making big promises about how easy the product was to sell and how much money I could make, but the furniture was battered, the carpets were worn, the ashtrays hadn't been emptied lately, and the man's clothing showed signs of wear, I knew not to believe a word I was hearing.

At last I spotted an ad from Trane, the heating and air-conditioning people. They were just opening a sales office in Cincinnati. What caught my eye was a line in the ad that said, "Guaranteed $25,000 a year." They were polite enough to interview me, though I suspect it was a struggle to keep from laughing at the idea that this plucky schoolboy thought he was qualified to work for an established, eminent company like Trane. Then came the showdown: "We're hiring full-time people who can be out making sales calls while you're sitting in a classroom, and there's a weeklong training program."

I said, "I've run my own business; I've sold door-to-door—fifteen, eighteen units a week. I will guarantee you that within a month I will be in the top tier of your salespeople." I was walking a fine line. If I sounded too confident, I'd come across as a blowhard. Not confident enough, and they would remain determined to show me the door.

"And I'll get excused from school to attend the training."

Finally one of the guys said, "You know what—what the hell? Letting you sit through the training won't cost us much of anything."

At the end of training, they gave each of the six new salesmen two leads—two families to visit. I came back the next day with orders for two $3,500 systems. Everybody else came back empty-handed. At the end of the first month, I was their number-one salesman, and I remained number one right through the end of high school and into the summer months before I was to start college.

I had graduated third in a class of over 250 and been offered full academic scholarships (tuition, room, board, and books) at two schools, choosing to go to the local one, the University of Cincinnati. At that time, thirty thousand students were enrolled. With thirty hours of college credit thanks to the advanced studies program at Purcell, bolstered by a university equivalency test, I was able to start as a third-quarter freshman.

By the time I entered college, I was living in my own apartment, driving my own new car, and earning more money than many graduates. I ended the first term on the dean's list, with a 3.85 grade point average.

Through that summer of 1976, the now-familiar feeling of "I can do better than this" began gnawing at me. I decided to start my own business. The math was simple: on a furnace that a customer would shell out $1,700 for, the cost of goods was about $350, with another $100 for additional materials and $200 for the installer. There was a good $1,000 profit to be made. The Trane units carried a higher price tag, but they were handing me only about $170 in commission for each sale. I could be selling the same three units a week and clearing maybe $2,000, instead of $500 in commissions.

I guess the people at Trane weren't very happy about losing their number-one salesman. My eleven months there had provided me a good education in the business. Full of enthusiasm, I went to see the local Carrier representative. He told me, "You'll never make it. I've seen a hundred guys try." Then he said, "Are you Charlie Harrington's son? Does your father own MLT?"

Yes, Charlie was my father. "I had my first beer at eighteen at the Mt. Lookout Tavern. Let me help you out here. But trust me; it's a tough business. In ninety days I won't be hearing from you anymore. You're going to be done."

Businessman

To make my start-up company sound prosperous and well-established, I picked the name "Tri-State Heating" (Cincinnati standing near a corner of Ohio that borders Indiana and Kentucky). That name was already registered but hadn't been used in some years. I tracked down the man who owned the name and offered to buy it from him; he was retired and perhaps lonely, and said, "I'll sell you the name for a dollar if you let me go out on jobs with you sometimes." Fair enough. To every local who recognized the name, it gave the air that we had been in business for twenty-five years.

I hired a telemarketer to make phone calls to people who had just bought a home. Again the hook was something free. She'd call and say, "We're offering a free furnace cleaning and free energy check. We have a guy who's going to be in your neighborhood next Tuesday." Well more than half the time, the homeowner wouldn't have a clue about how to check whether his furnace needed a cleaning and would be glad to accept the offer. When we went in, the technician might find, for example, that the furnace used a pilot light. I'd bring down the owner and explain that he could save 17 to 20 percent on his heating bill with a furnace that used a spark ignition instead of the pilot light. With bank financing already lined up, I could show the homeowner how he could get into a new furnace for only $30 a month, saving enough money in a year and a half to pay for the cost of the furnace. "And by the way," I'd say, "while we're at it, we could add air-conditioning, which we can offer you at our special winter off-season rates."

I started reading every book on salesmanship I could get my hands on, teaching myself how to handle every sales objection.

Most salespeople who visit the home will make a sales pitch just to the husband, if the wife isn't home. But that makes it too easy for him to say, "I've got to talk to my wife about it," leaving the salesperson to walk out empty-handed. I learned to get around that by starting out with, "Maybe we should wait until your wife is available." This would usually bring a reply of "It's okay. I make the decisions about things like this." In saying that, he had already denied himself one of the easiest excuses for not buying.

Maybe you'll think this next one is manipulative. I see it as a way to help people make a decision they already want to make. If I had the husband and wife together but they seemed indecisive, I'd sometimes ask them, "Are you the kind of people who make decisions, or do you want to get advice from your parents?" Of course, no self-respecting householder wants to admit that he has to consult with Daddy before he makes a purchase.

By law, consumers have a three-day rescission period. At Trane, something like 20 or 30 percent of the sales got canceled. I learned how to help people make sure they were doing the right thing. Walking toward the door, their check in hand, I'd stop and turn around and say, "Wait a minute. I just need another minute. I hate doing this but I have to ask—if there's any chance you're going to change your mind, please take the check back right now."

I'd insist they take the check from me, and then I'd spend three or four minutes going over all the terms of the deal. The householder would assure me that those were the terms as he understood them, and give me back the check.

Occasionally some sixth sense would tell me that my customer was still having a few misgivings. My approach at that critical point was to give him back the check a second time, insisting he take it, and go through all the terms once again, until he was clearly convinced he was doing the right thing, making a good decision.

I never had a single cancellation.

Signing up four or five jobs a week, I had to pay in advance for that many furnaces and installations, an outlay of some $15,000 or $20,000. But I had started the company with only $3,000. The prediction that I would last ninety days suddenly seemed too optimistic. Still, sales were going fine. The entrepreneurial side of me said, *Go for it. You're going to be successful.*

I went in to talk to the local Westinghouse representative. On the basis of the sales I was getting, he overlooked my age and agreed to let me have $150,000 of inventory on a consignment basis. Every week, people from Westinghouse Credit would come to the place I was using for storage to inventory their merchandise. These guys would climb on top of every box, count every single piece, and present me an invoice, and I would write them a check on the spot for every unit I had sent out to a job site. I never missed a beat with them, and in time improved my situation with an additional $150,000 credit from another supplier, so I could build the business beyond what the Westinghouse arrangement allowed.

⌐I did something rather innovative that my competitors didn't like: I took out a full-page advertisement in the Yellow Pages that listed an office on the east side of Cincinnati, and another office on the west side, while every other heating/air-conditioning company had only one location and one phone number. I was *the* citywide company. In fact, our "westside office" was just an answering service taking telephone messages. From the start, we appeared to be a big company. We carried the best products as a dealer for Carrier, Fedders, and Bryant.⌐

When I did a sales call and the customer would say, "I can't afford it," I would say, "No problem; what can you afford? Can you afford $48 a month for forty-eight months?" And I would write them up that night. We would take their credit application, finance it at a local bank, and the bank would pay us cash.

In the heating and air-conditioning industry, summer produces about 80 percent of the profit for almost every company because every home and apartment building already had a furnace, but they didn't all have air-conditioning. In the winter, I had telemarketing people call homeowners and quote an off-season price for a furnace, or a furnace/air conditioner combination. We were selling as much air-conditioning in the wintertime as we were in the summer. Even better, in the wintertime people didn't shop price for air-conditioning, so our profit margins were higher.

By the end of my first year in business, my new company had a staff of twenty-five employees, and we had sold $1 million worth of air conditioners and furnaces. I was nineteen years old.

Someone with a different personality would probably still be running that same business. But another opportunity was soon calling, one that would lead me in a different direction, on a course to help launch an industry.

2

EN ROUTE

Perseverance . . . overcomes almost everything.

—John D. Rockefeller

Picture a fresh-faced college student who attends class until 1:00 PM every day and then hurries across town, puts on a different hat, and spends the next nine hours running his million-dollar company.

I signed up to take a class called Orientation to Business. When I showed up for the first session, I couldn't believe what I was seeing. It was in a large lecture hall, crammed with what must have been about fifteen hundred students, chattering, laughing, throwing paper airplanes—mayhem.

Class started, not with the professor striding to the lectern, but with his image projected onto a screen, apologizing for not being there in person but promising he would be with us "most of the time." Somehow that wasn't reassuring. Another course in my business program at the University of Cincinnati,

Salesmanship, was taught by a professor who had virtually no selling experience. Overall, the business program was a big disappointment. I'm sure it's better now, and even back then the other students were probably getting more out of it than I was.

I decided to drop out. Because of those advanced-placement courses in high school, I was listed as being in my junior year. Another year and a half and they would have handed me a degree. Patience has never been one of my great virtues.

My mother was very upset with me about quitting college, but my dad, who was by then retired from the restaurant business and had joined me as my right-hand man in the heating/air-conditioning firm, told me, "If you don't quit college, I'm going to quit working for you." Even though I had been calling in between each of my morning classes and spending every afternoon and evening in the office, the hectic pace and constant need for right-now decisions was proving more than he wanted to continue to juggle. He wanted me there full time.

If I had it to do over again, my decision to quit college would be the same. But it's just because that's the kind of guy I am. For my son, I'd be very unhappy if he didn't finish. Except for a youngster as driven as I was, getting a college degree is, of course, the only way to go.

So at age twenty-one, I became a full-time businessman running my own company, with six trucks and cash flow that most small business owners would give their eye teeth for. I bought myself a Thunderbird, and I bought myself a house. Nothing fancy, but it was on the good side of town, on Laverty Lane in Anderson

Township, not too far from where I had grown up. Payments on the $38,000 mortgage came to $290 a month. A friend moved into one of the four bedrooms, paying me $300 a month in rent.

Most of my competitors in the heating business were men who had started out as installers. Compared to me, they couldn't sell worth a damn. They were getting frustrated trying to figure out how this upstart company could be bringing in so many customers. But they understood the hands-on part of the business, the part that I was a dummy about. It didn't help that I was a little lax in checking the credentials of the contract installers we were hiring.

At first, about 20 percent of our jobs didn't pass city inspection. When the Inspection Department caught on that our people weren't doing good work, they started coming down hard on us. We had to beef up the service department and make sure we were hiring people who knew what they were doing. Still, it's quite a challenge to judge the quality of workmanship and whether a job has been done correctly when you're mostly in the dark about how it's supposed to be done. We had five or six crews; of those, only one or two were top quality.

I wasn't cut out for the service end of the business. As a salesman, I didn't like all those return trips to the customer, with them telling me that the house didn't get hot enough or the furnace was too noisy. I found myself wondering what I was doing in the heating business.

My sister Salli called one day in the middle of a cold, dry Cincinnati winter. She and her husband were going on a trip, and she wanted a humidifier installed on the furnace while they were away. This was a pretty routine job. We had done lots of them. When they got back home, they found a disaster. The wiring had been done incorrectly, the furnace had shut down, and water had spread everywhere . . . until the pipes had frozen.

For me, it was the last straw. I had never managed to get my arms around the installation side of the business, and I had never developed a knack for hiring reliable installers. My staff was a rag-tag assortment of what we used to call "jack-legs"—incompetent blowhards who came in with stories of how experienced they were and all the great work they had done on their last job, and then likely to turn out to be drunks, thieves, or both. I fired the useless guy who botched my sister's job. She was furious. Her husband, a lawyer, told me, "We'll never do business with your company again." At least he didn't threaten to sue. But the embarrassment shook me. It was the tipping point. I didn't think the frustrations were worth it anymore. A few months earlier, when some of us had been sitting around shooting the breeze, I had said something like, "Someday, I'm going to sell this place."

One of the guys had said, "Yeah? When? I'd be a buyer if you did."

Remembering that, I went to him and said, "Make me an offer." We negotiated a price, I gave part of the money to my dad, and I walked away.

WHAT NEXT?

Beginning a search for a business that I truly wanted to be in was like opening a door and stepping out into a fresh spring breeze. I was still hardly more than a kid, single, and with a net worth of something like $75,000 if you included the equity in my house. The experiences of getting my feet wet in several different businesses had given me a good education in what I didn't want to do. The restaurant business? Too many uncertainties, and only the brilliant or the lucky get rich. The paving business? That had been okay when I was a teen. The air-conditioning and heating business? Been there, done that.

The local newspapers and the entrepreneur magazines were filled with ads promoting all kinds of business opportunities. Scouring them like a sailor in a lifeboat searching the horizon for signs of a ship, I took notes on anything that looked halfway likely. I discovered there were brokers who specialized in match-making between people trying to sell a business and people looking for one to buy.

And then there were all the franchises looking to gain a foothold in the Cincinnati market—delis and pizza parlors, the chicken chain Chick-fil-A, home improvement outfits offering a service or a custom product like stained-glass overlays, cleaning operations like Stanley Steamer, and on and on. Many of these were being offered through brokers. I looked at forty or fifty, each time hoping the next one would light a spark, then pouring through their business plans and financial statements, meeting with the owners, and facing the reality that this one wasn't any more promising than the others.

Every time, I'd ask myself, *Can I really see coming in here every day and watching over meat slicers or guys making corned beef sandwiches?* Nothing got me excited. I had been poring through the books and records, the brochures, marketing materials, and videos, looking at the headaches of the businesses, worrying over the sweaty hours that the would-be sellers were putting in. Okay, I was only twenty-two, but I had been around the block a few times already. I had enough business experience under my belt to know about the labor problems, the theft problems, and so on. I wanted to do something big—not look over the shoulder of teens making pizzas or brawny guys cutting up pieces of colored glass. Frustrated with what I was finding in my hometown, I started looking nationally, poring over the business ads in *USA Today*, the *Wall Street Journal*, the *New York Times*, and *Entrepreneur* magazine.

Not that my money was running out—I still had plenty and was marshalling it carefully—but living in the limbo of not having a business to wake up to every morning was unfamiliar territory, and uncomfortable as hell. My mother was tickled with my siblings—my brother an executive at Gillette, one of my sisters married to a doctor, the other to a lawyer. And then there was Kevin, who at the moment had no occupation, no income, no prospects, and no idea what he wanted to do. My days had been full, my life fulfilled. Now my days were busy with nothing more than a big hunt. Life felt empty.

So while continuing to search, I signed up to take on the

Cincinnati distributorship for a multilevel marketing outfit called NaturSlim. Similar to Herbalife that would come along a few years later, NaturSlim offered a line of weight-loss products sold friend-to-friend and door-to-door. This was a part-time business for me. Still, before long I had expanded to a five-state area and became the leading distributor. I signed up so many subdistributors that the number still amazes me: at the end, I had five thousand of them.

After about a year, the company announced that it had decided to offer a similar line of products through retail channels. The friend-to-friend sales model quickly collapsed. Though I was devastated and felt betrayed, I was in a healthy condition financially. It was my franchisees who were hurting. They had believed in the business because of me. Many of them thought I was part of management and that I shared responsibility for the decision. My phone rang day and night with folks calling to complain, threaten, cajole. I tried to explain that I was getting screwed the same way they were, that my cash flow had collapsed just like theirs.

I thought it was pure greed that the company owners had turned their backs on all their franchisees and all the individuals who were out in the neighborhoods producing the company's revenue. So I wasn't exactly upset about the owners' fate when the company went under not long after.

I threw myself back into the search for a business. Whenever I found a proposition that looked promising, after I had talked to their people and examined their paperwork, I'd set out to talk with one or two of the franchisees to see the operation with my own eyes.

I began traveling feverishly.

To people who live on the coast, it can be eye-opening to discover how many cities are within a one-day drive for a midwesterner. I visited Toledo, Cleveland, Louisville, Columbus, St. Louis, Detroit, Nashville, Atlanta, plus others I don't even remember.

When the local pickings didn't seem to offer very much of interest, I expanded my horizons, packing a bag and hopping on an airplane to Denver, to San Francisco, to Minneapolis—to anywhere I came across an opportunity that sounded as if it might offer the magic combination: something I would find challenging enough to be satisfying and lucrative enough to be worth the effort by my already exaggerated demands.

After about a half a year of this without any success and without any letup, the search led me to a man named Neil Balter. By then I had grown sour on the idea of finding a franchise operation that would meet my ideals. He had started an outfit called the California Closet Company, in Woodland Hills, outside of Los Angeles. When I flew out to meet with him, I found a guy who looked like a true California type, a twenty-something surfer dude with long blonde hair.

Years later, Neil and I and a couple of other folks would get together to start the Young Entrepreneurs Organization. But that's getting ahead of the story.

Balter was about my age and had started his company by customizing his own closet, then doing others on contract, and he quickly recognized the larger opportunity. At the time, what would become a large national business was still in its infancy, with some eight or ten franchises then up and running. But Neil and his operation had the smell of success.

After he finished his pitch, I thought, *I'm like this guy. I'm a promoter, a marketer.* But I also thought, *I don't see myself owning one of these franchises. I see myself more like Neil, owning operations all over the country.* I told him, "I love what you're doing, but I see this as sort of downgrading myself back to the in-home selling of my rustproofing days."

Still, the concept appealed to me. Without even thinking it through, I said, "I have a great idea. I've spent months and months looking for the right business. You run these ads in *Entrepreneur* magazine and promote in all these other ways. You're looking for people to get into business with you, and I'm looking for a business to get into. Building closets isn't for me— I'm hungry for something that can be really big. Maybe I could be your East Coast guy."

I said, "Let me follow up on your leads in my part of the country and sell some franchises for you. Let me help you out in building your business until I find what I want to do."

He picked up the idea and ran with it. "The article they just did about me in *Entrepreneur* magazine led to four hundred phone calls from people interested in finding out about buying a franchise. I don't have the time to follow up on all this stuff." He went on, "One guy called from Dayton, another guy called from Cincinnati. It's a great idea for you to help me out here."

This could turn into a real opportunity to carry me over

while I continued looking for the right business. I asked him, "Neil, what would it be worth to you?"

Here was the kind of guy I could admire: he didn't even have to stop and think, much less scratch out some numbers on paper or pull out a calculator. "I charge $25,000 for a franchise fee. I'll feed you the leads I get in your part of the country. You follow up on them. For every one you work on who buys a franchise, I'll give you 20 percent of the franchise fee—five grand."

That sounded like something I could live with. But maybe it could be sweetened. "Let me ask you something," I said. "You're going to give me five or ten people to follow up on. Great. But what if I run ads and find people on my own instead of waiting for leads from you? What if I dig into my pocket and run some ads in the local newspapers?"

"If it's your own lead, I'll give you $8,000."

Just short of one-third of his franchise fee. That sounded pretty cool to me, and we shook hands on it.

I flew back to Cincinnati feeling very charged up.

What Neil Balter and I came up with sounded like the answer I had been searching for. Besides, here was a guy cut from the same block of wood as me: not just an entrepreneur but one who could recognize another entrepreneur. We had hit it off like old buddies.

So Neil and I drew up papers, signed them, and I threw myself into my new adventure. I began running ads that were pretty soon drawing hundreds of phone calls a month. *Hundreds.* A lot of the folks listened to the pitch and said something like, "That sounds pretty cool, but it isn't for me. I'm not real excited about being a closet guy. But if you run into anything else that looks interesting, let me know."

After a while, the last part of that began to capture my attention. I started thinking, *Jeez, if I'm going to represent California Closet, maybe I should be looking around for some other franchises I could represent.* Neil hadn't asked for an exclusive with me; I wouldn't have done the deal if he had insisted on that. While I continued to look for the right business for myself, I thought I might be able to sign up some other companies. I don't think I was cocky; I prefer to think of it as self-confidence based on what I had already achieved. In any case, I thought I might be able to sign up another thirty to forty businesses to represent. Somewhere along the line, I'd run into a franchise idea that lit my fire, and I'd buy one for myself. What kind of operation would it take to get me excited? I had no idea. But in the meantime, I'd be making a living selling other people's franchises.

Back when I had been running my heating company, I had bought a commercial building as a warehouse and offices. As part of the terms when I sold the company, the new owner agreed to lease the building from me—all except for some office space that I held back for my own use. Within a few months of my trip to meet with Neil Balter in California, I had two operations up and running out of those offices.

One was the Small Business Center. I began by running ads carefully honed to grab the attention of people looking for a business to buy. I had been reading these ads myself for months at this point and had a pretty good idea of what would work. It wasn't long before the calls were coming fast and furious. Then it was time to start calling up folks at some of the companies for sale and franchise outfits I had visited. "I've decided I'm not interested in what you've got," I'd tell them. "But I'm representing a couple of other deals. I'm running ads on a local level. Every week, we're getting hundreds of calls."

After explaining my deal with California Closets, my pitch would go something like this: "A lot of these people don't want to buy a closet franchise, but they may be interested in opening a Subway sandwich franchise" or whatever the business was of the person I was talking to.

The deal I would lay on the table was straightforward, very similar to the terms I had with Neil Balter on the California Closets deal. My services wouldn't cost them anything; they would only owe me money when I brought them someone who signed on for a franchise. They would pay me a percentage of their franchise fee as a commission, the figure usually ranging between 20 and 30 percent depending on the particular situation. "You don't pay me a nickel unless I bring you a deal," I'd tell them. In effect, I was acting as a franchise broker.

Then I took it a big step further by creating a brokerage business as well. I leased another entire floor of the office building and rented out space to agents and brokers for just about everything a small or start-up businessperson needs: in the one location, an entrepreneur could learn about franchise opportunities and local businesses for sale, discuss a business loan, arrange for business insurance, get help finding store or office space to rent, and more. Everybody fed business leads back and forth, paying commissions to each other. On top of brokering franchises, we could then help the buyer find a prize location and earn ourselves a real estate commission as well. If we negotiated a lease, we made money; if we handled the sale of a building, we made money; if we helped someone buy an existing business, we made money; and if clients didn't want to buy an existing business, we'd sell them a franchise, and make money. This we called the small business center.

THE BUSINESS OF SELLING BUSINESSES

The other company was the business that sold the franchises—not just in Cincinnati but throughout a good section of the Midwest, including Louisville, Lexington, Indianapolis, Toledo, Cleveland, Columbus, Pittsburgh, and a little bit in Detroit. The operation went like this: we'd advertise in the classified business-opportunity section of the newspapers: "Looking for a business to buy? Don't buy it until you come on down to the Holiday Inn and attend our free 'Own Your Own Business' franchise seminar."

We'd have six or eight franchise opportunities lined up, sometimes with the president or a key player from each on hand to make the pitch—though getting top people to fly in for any audience of twenty-five or fifty people wasn't always easy.

Whether a lucky guess or a brilliant flash of foresight, the franchise brokerage business proved to be an exciting and fulfilling period of my life. In time, we had hundreds of franchise companies under contract. We sold thousands of franchises and distributorships, running full-page ads in business magazines, going gangbusters, generating $5 million in transactions a year. I was rubbing shoulders with people like Freddy DeLuca at a time when he was trying to get a foothold with his Subway restaurants; today he's a billionaire.

Neil Balter would eventually sell California Closets to Williams Sonoma for something like $10 million. I was getting an education in lots of different businesses, poring over the books and records, forming a picture of the ups and the downs, learning how to build them, how to sell them, the art of selecting locations.

The name we came up with for this company was Franchise America. It might not have been the very first franchise brokerage company in America, but it was certainly a major player.

I had been hopping all around the Midwest, doing Dayton for breakfast and Toledo for lunch. I didn't mind the hard work and long hours—I had discovered at an early age that hard work was what kept my clock ticking. And I was living well, enjoying myself in my spare time, dancing the bachelors' dance, hanging my hat in a spacious apartment at One Lytle Place, the first high-rise condo building in downtown Cincinnati, right on the Ohio River. The building even offered an elevated walkway to Riverfront Stadium where the Bengals threw footballs in the cold months and the Cincinnati Reds threw baseballs in the warm ones.

It's been a lifelong pattern to work hard, but to play hard as well. Making friends has always been easy for me. Maybe all of that comes from being a bar owner's son. Half the players of both teams lived in my building. I got to know many of them and would often hang out with them at the local bars and night-clubs. The crowd also included lots of local reporters and tele-vision people, entertainers, and an assorted mix of nightclub characters. I got to know the fabled (later infamous) Pete Rose. He was wild even then; nobody thought much about it when we'd be with him at the racetrack, seeing him bet a few thou-sand dollars on several races in an afternoon. We didn't see it as a gambling problem, just "It's Pete Rose."

Another colorful character in that era of my life was the Cincinnati mayor whose name has since become familiar to many: Jerry Springer. His departure from politics was trig-gered by an incident he'd probably rather forget. A police raid on a bawdy house across the river in Kentucky turned up a check he had written, made out to the management. On the other hand, he may very well have had a much more success-ful career because of that incident; for all I know, he looks back on it as a happy turning point in his life.

In 1984, during the Reagan administration, the Federal Com-munications Commission deregulated television advertising. Overnight, networks and local stations were no longer limited to seven minutes of advertising for each thirty minutes of broadcast. Viewers didn't see any sudden change, though. Broadcast executives were smart enough to realize that slashing program content to run an extra few minutes of commercials would likely drive audiences away.

But for me, I was struck by what seemed a lightning bolt of inspiration. I thought about those newspaper ads I'd been using as my net to round up potential buyers—*Print is so static*, I now began to think. *It doesn't move, doesn't talk, doesn't show the franchise, and it sure doesn't convey emotion. Instead of just "Come down to the Holiday Inn and hear about it," how about if I showed* it?

That pitch I had been giving in front of a handful of people at a time sitting on uncomfortable hotel chairs—was it possible I could condense it into a short video, with footage of the franchise in action, and show it on television?

My life was about to change.

3

AN INDUSTRY IS BORN

*If we did all the things we are capable of,
we would astound ourselves.*

—Thomas Edison

The company providing the cable TV service to my condo building was Warner Amex Cable. I noticed that channel 28 on their system was a display of classified ads—no video, no photographs, not even sketches, nothing but text. They had simply lifted the concept of newspaper classified ads and put them on the air. It was completely static, totally boring, with not even the slightest attempt to reach the viewers' emotions.

That was on channel 28. And what was on channel 29? Exactly the same thing: static classified ads just as in a newspaper, many of them identical to the ads on channel 28. I called the local Warner offices, asked for the ad sales department, and said to the man who answered, "I don't know if there's something wrong with my TV, but . . . ," and explained about the duplication.

"No," the man said. "It's not a mistake. We're required to have a certain number of channels on the air, and we don't have enough programming to fill them all." A few days later I was at their Blue Ash building, sitting across the table from the manager of their advertising sales. I told him, "I'll give you videos to run on channel 29 and pay you for the airtime." In those early days, virtually all the revenue for cable TV was coming from subscribers; if you came in with money to spend for advertising, they loved you.

He asked me, "Do you have any production experience?" No, but I had found out that they were required to provide what's called "local access"—allowing local businesspeople and citizens to get some airtime and production at extremely low rates. I said, "I don't, but do you have production facilities I could use?" He answered, "As a matter of fact, we do." I already knew that. I asked him to make me a proposal. He talked to his management, came back, and said, "We'll produce your show in our studios. We've got airtime to fill, so we'll run each one of your programs thirty times."

"For how much?"

"Eight hundred dollars," he said. *Eight hundred dollars!* That included studio time, crew, cameras, lighting, time in the editing bay, *and* thirty airings! Fantastic. I was blown away. (What's incredible is that this rule is *still* in effect across the country for many local cable stations. Even today, I buy half hours of time on local cable stations on Saturday mornings for $100. Somehow, very few people seem to know about this amazing advertising opportunity.)

My aim was to produce half-hour shows featuring ten local folks who had a business to sell—a pizza parlor, a bar, a laundromat, a gas station, or whatever. It's like the shows you can see on local television today that feature homes for sale. I'd interview one person on camera and roll clips of his business from his video reel, then move on to the next. An attractive young anchor lady from the local NBC station agreed to appear on camera to do the openings and closings of *American Dream—The Own Your Own Business Show*, which is what we had decided to call the program. She charged me all of $250 per program.

After the first show, it was clear that so many different stories in a single half hour was overkill—a typical business viewer would have trouble sorting out that many offerings, when only one or two might be of real interest. By the second or third program, we had revamped to do only three segments of about ten minutes each.

The trouble was that if we got Joe's Pizza Parlor as a client, as soon as he found a buyer he, of course, wasn't interested in being on the show anymore. Worse, sometimes we'd get calls to say, "I'm swamped with so many leads that it'll take me weeks to follow up on them. Take me off the air." We had to keep coming up with new clients. So how about going after the Neil Balters, the owners of national franchise operations?

Within about two months, I had a second weekly show running in tandem, under the Franchise America banner. Where *American Dream* mostly sold individual businesses in

Cincinnati, the new show was suited to a vastly larger market-place—offering messages to tempt would-be entrepreneurs into opening a California Closets franchise or whatever in their own hometown.

In those early days, national sponsors weren't buying advertising time during the sleep hours, so the cable companies would go off air at midnight: they could hardly give the time away. Every place I wanted to be had channel space available, and I had no problem buying up half-hour blocks of cable television time in over two hundred cities. Instead of shutting down at midnight, these companies would sell me their overnight time for as little as I was paying for local access.

The franchise companies featured on the show would pay me five dollars for the name, address, and phone number of each person who called in, and I would often get hundreds of phone calls from a single airing. That was on top of the fee they paid to be on the show. And of course I also got a percentage of every franchise they sold from one of my leads.

Now I could run the same ad in the newspapers, but instead of saying, "Come down to the Holiday Inn," I'd say, "Turn on your TV at 7:00 tonight." And instead of twenty-five people showing up, I'd get an audience of thousands and two or three hundred phone calls.

At first I was charging $5,000 to $7,500 to be on the show, which covered my costs for rental of camera and lights, the camera crew, videotape, editing, and so on, and we'd give companies a copy of the tape afterward to use in their own promotions.

Before long, each show was generating an astounding number of leads: *tens of thousands*. What had started out as a way of arranging things so I didn't have to travel so much and could reach wider audiences was turning into a very handsome profit center.

Booking time on separate television stations all over the Midwest became a headache. It made sense to see if I could work out a deal with one of the national cable channels. I got in touch with the Discovery Channel, which, like the local outlets, was dark at night for lack of programming and lack of advertising. They were happy to sell me late-night airtime. For a half hour on the Discovery Channel nationwide, back in 1984 and '85, they were charging me a flat fee of . . . $100.

Finding new franchise operators to sign up was a no-brainer. I'd go to the business opportunity shows, where there might be a hundred different people selling franchises. On the first day, I'd go from booth to booth. I'd invite everybody who understood the potential of advertising on television up to the suite I had rented and run one of our programs for them. Before the tape was even finished, at least one person in the group would say something like, "Can I be on that show?" By then the Franchise America program was running on television stations all over the Midwest, and our fee had gone up to $10,000 for each segment; the higher charges made possible better production values, footage shot on the client's location, better editing, and so on.

Over the next two days, right in my suite, I'd shoot a video segment with each of the people who had signed up. On a single weekend, I might videotape ten or fifteen interviews, enough for three or four programs. By the time I packed my suitcase on Sunday evening, I would often have checks and credit card receipts totaling more than $30,000.

By then I had already started a lifelong practice of haunting the trade shows to look for products. I'd see a tape of our production running in various people's booths, with a banner reading, "As seen on the Franchise America show."

I still have videotapes of some of those early shows, but don't ask to see them. Though they were making me tons of money, they were pretty dreadful, with no sizzle at all. Today I wouldn't screen them for my closest friends.

Fun Raisers

Not having to travel so much gave me time to enjoy a better social life. One of the young women I knew at that time, Peggy Krantz, talked to me about an idea she had of starting a singles club. She was recently divorced and wasn't meeting the kind of people she wanted to be with. I liked the idea—to me it sounded like a good way of expanding my circle of fun and interesting people. I invited some friends, she invited some, and the friends invited friends. We named our group Cincinnati Fun Raisers. And, yes, it was an intentional play on "fund-raisers," since we wanted to set loftier goals than just getting together to drink and dance. In 1983 we put on a large evening function, with proceeds going to the Cincinnati Children's Hospital cancer research program. Of all the things I've done in my life, one that

I am very proud of is Fun Raisers: after twenty-five years, the group is still in existence, still holding its annual benefit ball, and has donated $500,000 to Children's Hospital to fight children's cancer and blood disorders.

ANOTHER NEW DIRECTION

In 1985, at one of those weekend trade shows for entrepreneurs where I drummed up business, a keynote address was given by a man named Ron Smith, who was then the editor of *Entrepreneur* magazine. It turned out that the magazine had published an extensive series of *How to Start a Business* manuals. I had never sold a product on television, just businesses and franchises, but it struck me that this might be an opportunity. After his speech, I went over and introduced myself, telling him that I wanted to buy large quantities of their manuals at a wholesale price. He liked the idea enough to say, "You should come out and talk to our publisher."

In short order I was on an airplane to the company offices in Los Angeles. Now, I had sized up the somewhat disheveled Ron Smith as friendly and brainy, what I thought of as a "writer type." I was smart enough myself not to be intimidated by his intellect. With his publisher, though, I didn't know what to expect. You have to understand that I was twenty-seven at this time but still looked a good deal younger than my age. In fact, I probably didn't look a day over eighteen. For important meetings—and this one was important to me—I always dressed up to look as much as I could like a prosperous businessman: dress shirt and tie and a really snappy suit. Maybe it didn't actually make me look any older, but it added to my confidence, and I needed all the help I could get.

Their offices turned out to be in a commercial district, and the building looked as if it might have been converted from a warehouse. I had gotten all dressed up for *this*? It was hardly what I expected. (I would find out later that the company had been through bankruptcy, which probably explained its down-scale base of operations.)

The publisher, Wellington Ewen, turned out to be a financial guy, a banker type who had been brought in to put the operation back on a sound footing. With his polished style and his walrus mustache, sitting in his large, imposing office, I took him for a blue blood. This was clearly a man pleased with new ideas and interested in any solid scheme that could contribute to cash flow. He and Ron Smith, who was also in the meeting, seemed fascinated by my background and what I was accomplishing. By the time we were through talking, Ewen and I had agreed to the general terms for my selling their *How to Start a Business* books on television.

This was one time when my youthful good looks might have turned out to be an advantage. Ron Smith said to me, "Wow, what you're doing is amazing. You're a true small-business entrepreneur. We'll do this deal, and we'll put you in the magazine."

The November 1985 issue of *Entrepreneur* featured me on the cover and carried a flattering story about me. I tried not to let it all go to my head. My mother, who I'm afraid was still uncertain I would ever amount to anything, was finally beginning to get the idea that I might not end up destitute after all. I got well over a thousand phone calls as a result of the story, and countless people showed up at the door with a product tucked under their arm.

Meanwhile I had heard the music of the enchantress who makes people from cold climates fall in love with the sunny skies and warm weather of Southern California. A friend of a friend had a three-bedroom condo near where Sunset Boulevard meets the Pacific Coast Highway ("PCH," to the locals). It was close to Santa Monica and Malibu, minutes from the wide, miles-long sandy beaches where the young and not so young of Los Angeles show off their tans and their hard bodies. I kept my home in Cincinnati but rented a room in the condo to use whenever I could find an excuse to go to California.

As soon as I was settled in the condo, I started tackling the sale of the *How to Start a Business* books on television. I had by then done hundreds and hundreds of half-hour TV shows featuring franchises and businesses for sale. What was different about this one was that it wasn't for a franchise or business. It was for a product.

A SHORT-TERM PARTNERSHIP

A man named Beryl Wolk, who had seen the article in *Entrepreneur*, had a staffer call me. Beryl was operating out of

Philadelphia, publishing *Cable Guide Magazine,* a television guide for cable channels that he was selling by subscription to 10 million households. He had a small challenge on his hands that he thought I might be able to help with to our mutual advantage. He was carrying full-page ads from Lifetime, the Discovery Channel, and others, but they weren't paying him in cash. Instead he had agreed to take their ads on a barter basis: they were paying him in credits for late-night airtime on their networks.

In 1986, when he approached me, Beryl was generating credits for hundreds of hours *a week* in airtime. He proposed turning the airtime credits over to me in exchange for his becoming half owner of Franchise America. I saw it as an attractive step up: Beryl struck me as one of the most brilliant idea people I had ever met, and he had connections that could be very valuable for Franchise America. A partnership with him would put me in the big leagues. And he was willing to put money into Franchise America, tens of thousands of dollars initially, which would put us on a more solid footing.

We agreed on terms, the lawyers drew up the paperwork, and Beryl and I were in business together. I continued to run Franchise America; his staff kept the books and paid the bills. Being in the same town as my new partner made sense to me, so I packed up my belongings and moved my operation to suburban Philly. You won't be surprised to learn, though, that I didn't give up my room near the beach in Los Angeles.

Doorway to the Birth of an Industry

One day in 1987, a jovial, friendly supersalesman named Charles Hall walked into my office, plopped down a gadget, and announced it would be a great product to sell on television. He gave me a pitch on the device that they were calling the "Food Saver."

"For example," he said, "when you buy bacon at the supermarket, you're paying about six dollars a pound. When you have a food sealer, you instead go to a bulk-food store and buy your bacon in a five-pound block. You take it home and cut it up into chunks of about twelve ounces each. One of them you put in your refrigerator to use as you need. The others you shrink wrap with the Food Saver using the plastic bags that come with it—cutting your bill for that item by 50 percent."

I asked him to hang on for a minute, went out into the hall and grabbed staffer Milt LaFair, telling him, "There's this wild man sitting in my office. You gotta go talk to him. I need a break. Go listen to him, and I'll join you shortly."

A few minutes later, Milt came looking for me. He said, "Kevin, you have to come in here and check this out."

I went back in, and the man demonstrated for me what Milt had already seen. To show how powerful his unit was, he took an empty Coke can and put it into one of his wrappers, stuck the open end of the wrapper into the food sealer and turned it on. The gadget sucked out all the air so effectively that the Coke can collapsed as if it had been crushed.

I was blown away by the demo and his story . . . until I asked what he thought the device and the wrappings should sell for.

"Three hundred dollars," he said.

I almost laughed in his face.

But the more we talked, the more I understood how quickly a family would save back the cost of the product and then keep on saving. And the more I understood, the more I was convinced that this could be a successful product to sell on television, the same way we had sold the *How to Start a Business* books.

⌊Within a couple of days, I had a deal in place. We moved fast: the commercial for the Food Saver was on the air a month later.⌉

You may already know about the Food Saver; if you don't, you certainly know some people who do. The product turned out to be a huge winner, giving us many millions of dollars in sales. It would take its place as the longest-running product in what would become the "infomercial" business, and our all-time number-one seller. (In those early days, when someone asked what field I was in, I said I was in the "sellavision" business. Curiously, no one knows where the term "infomercial" came from. Someone must have coined it, but no one knows who.)

Yet even though we earned a true fortune on this product, there is a downside to the story. The agreement we made gave us exclusive TV rights. That's what I was focused on; that's the business I was in—that's all that I was thinking about.

The infomercials made the product a national phenomenon, setting up the owners of Food Saver in time to make the move into retail on their own—without us.

Today, our agreements give us a piece of the business in every market. But our agreement on the Food Saver, which didn't address anything but television, meant we received no income from retail sales. We lost out on revenues approaching a billion dollars as a result of not having included in our contract the rights to every possible market.

The moral is obvious:

> When you make a deal for rights, try your best for an agreement that covers every potential source of income.

I now recognize the Food Saver as the show that carried me through a magic doorway into what would come to be called the infomercial business. At the time, it had seemed to me like nothing more than the next logical step.

BUILDING THE BUSINESS

With the challenge of keeping so many balls in the air at the same time, I talked to the guy I trusted most about coming to work with me: my brother Tim. Nine years younger, he was still in his junior year at University of Cincinnati. My mother had never forgiven me for dropping out of college. Neither of us held a college degree; she had always believed you couldn't be a success in life without that piece of paper.

Generally speaking, of course, I know she was right: the data clearly shows that college graduates take home a paycheck about twice as fat as those without a degree. Even though my parents could see I was living very well despite not having a college education, here I was asking Tim to become a dropout like me. They wanted him to finish college first. They were just about ready to kill me for offering him the job and just about ready to kill Tim for taking it.

On the hunt for a continuing flow of new products worthy of building an infomercial around, I bought a copy of the *Directory of Mail Order Catalogs* and sent out letters saying, "I'm an avid buyer from mail-order catalogs. I'm not currently getting yours. Please put me on your mailing list." What most people call "junk mail" is to me a source of business.

At the peak, I was receiving some two thousand catalogs. In the early years, I probably put in as many hours a week studying those catalogs as most people put in on their full-time jobs—even though the catalog reading was something I only found time for in the evening and on weekends. Today I still receive over five hundred catalogs, and I still go through them looking for products.

After our early successes with product infomercials like the Food Saver, I began to notice that other people were reading the same catalogs I was and producing the same type of shows. And not just infomercial companies: manufacturers like Sunbeam and Hamilton Beach at first couldn't figure out why the sales of their kitchen mixers suddenly spiked upward by 600 percent. The reason was one I hadn't even anticipated myself. Later, when a mixer of ours started airing, the product was only available through the 800-number given in the infomercial. But lots of people who saw the show didn't call the 800-number; instead, they hurried out to a local store to pick up whatever kitchen mixer they could find. Our show was bumping up the sales of every brand of mixer!

This was good news for the other manufacturers but brought a new challenge for us. It created all that much more incentive for infomercial producers. The competition was heating up; the field was becoming more competitive.

The go-getter Sam Catanese was one of the first people I used as a producer of our infomercials. One day I said to him, "Sam, I'm finding some of our competitors are running the same shows several times on a weekend. If we started taping the shows, we could keep track of which ones are getting a lot of play. And those are the products that are selling well. I'd like to start taping the airwaves. Can you do that for me?"

What's now called "monitoring," Sam Catanese began doing for me with ten videotape machines. By the end of the first year, he was recording with sixty of the units. Each night his machines would tape every cable channel that was running infomercials. In the morning, a bunch of college co-eds would come in to scan the tapes and make notes on what time each infomercial aired, how long it ran, and what product it was promoting. Those reports, now called "overnights," have become standard in the industry.

We assigned a numerical value to each time slot: a show that ran at 8:30 in the morning was more valuable than one that ran in the middle of the night. But our real focus of interest was on a show that somebody was running heavily—say, three times in a single night; it meant the company was doing what we came to call a "rollout." They knew they had a winner.

Through the years, I've been the springboard for many guys like Sam. They came to work for us, thought they saw a future on their own, and they left with our blessings and good wishes.

Sam called his new company Infomercial Monitoring Service, and it has made him a very rich man. He not only still produces overnights for the entire industry, but has a library of practically every product show and infomercial through the years—the largest such library on the face of the planet. When a Procter and Gamble wants to see the video on, say, every hair product ever featured in an infomercial, it's Sam they call.

Walking Away from Wolk

My deal with Philadelphia businessman Beryl Wolk taught me a costly lesson. Franchise America grew briskly with me running the business and my partner handling the finances. That arrangement made good sense to me when he first proposed it, since he had so many more years of experience with spreadsheets, cash flow, payrolls, and taxes than I did.

But in the Franchise America part of the business, we were supposed to be equal partners. I was bringing in 90 percent of the revenues but being paid like a salaried employee. I kept trying to talk to Beryl but was getting nowhere. My business abilities had taken a great stride just from working so close to this marketing wizard. Still, it was time to be on my own.

It was time to walk away.

⌐ If you plan to build a big business with another person, spend the time—and the legal fees—to work out every detail of the agreement. Dot every i and cross every t. And never enter an important deal without spelling out an exit strategy that lets either of you terminate the arrangement and lays out the terms of the split. ⌐

Without yet announcing my plans, I formed a new company and went out to hunt for office space. Blessed once again with uncanny luck, Tim and I stumbled into a gold mine—a suite of offices that had been rented by a company that had just gone bankrupt. They had cleared out only the week before, leaving behind telephones, a bunch of furniture, even pictures on the wall and a few plants.

Just one small problem: we would be starting out with a total staff of three people—the two of us and the secretary we had just hired—but the suite was designed for about twenty. We needed about fifteen hundred square feet; this place was four times too big. The landlord made a business decision that left us smiling. Figuring that any tenant was better than none and sizing us up as young, eager, and with good prospects, he took a chance. He said, "If you sign up for the whole space, I'll let you have everything that's here." Since the previous tenants had broken their lease, by law everything they left behind belonged to him. With at least as much confidence in our future as the trusting landlord, we jumped at the deal, even though the cost was way more than we should have been paying.

At certain moments in an entrepreneur's life, you get a gut feeling that something is about to break loose: you're about to take a risk that's going to be an essential step in climbing the ladder of success. This was one of those times.

On a Friday in August 1988, I told my partner in Franchise America that I was leaving, signed the lease for our new office space the same afternoon, and called the telephone company to have our phones turned on by Monday morning. I was in business for myself, as Quantum Marketing International Inc. QMI started off with a modest stake of $25,000 of my own money, a much too expensive lease, the salary for one secretary, and not a single client, not a dime of income. I was thirty-two years old.

Monday morning we arrived at the offices full of vigor and ready to start. The secretary came in, looked around, and said, "Where is everybody?" We explained that, for the moment, there wasn't anybody else. She left for lunch and never came back, explaining by phone, full of mistrust about what we were up to, that "You obviously have no business, and I don't want to be around there." Her reluctance didn't dampen our enthusiasm, but we still smile over her suspicions.

It makes me laugh now when I think about those offices. Tim and I installed ourselves at the far end of the suite. We left the names of all the former employees on the doors. Anybody coming to visit had to walk down a long corridor past these closed doors that made it look as if we had a large team of folks busy at work.

I had high hopes and great expectations, but I could hardly envision what lay ahead.

4

FROM ZERO TO WOW

Desire is the key to motivation, but it's
the determination and commitment
to an unrelenting pursuit of your goal—
a commitment to excellence—that will
enable you to attain the success you seek.

—Mario Andretti

My goal for the new company was captured in the head-line of the recruiting ads we started running in *USA Today* and the *Wall Street Journal*: "Help Us Find the Next Million-Dollar Product."

Hiring good salespeople in my circumstances wasn't easy. People would call and want to know: "Do you have health care? What about vacations? What's the salary?" And I'd have to lay it on the line: commissions only, no salary. My stock answer was, "We have plenty of benefits. We'll give you a desk, a phone, heating and air conditioning, travel expenses to the shows, and lots of leads." It took three weeks to hire the first handful of people. In the long run, though, quite a few of our salespeople made millions.

At the same time, we were putting out the word to a lot of our old contacts about the kinds of products we were looking for. As you've no doubt gathered by now from my stories of reading catalogs and attending trade shows looking for new products, I was and still am a rabid workaholic.

I only recommend this for people as driven as I am. A sixteen-hour workday is hell on your private life; it brought a lot of complaints from my first wife in the few years we spent together, and from girlfriends after that, but I have finally found a happy solution.

At a football game in 2004, I waved to a friend a couple of rows in front of me and then noticed one of the ladies she was with. Nobody had to tell me this gal who caught my eye was a model: it showed in her glow and her style. I pursued her for weeks with the same kind of determination that has served me well in business. The more she stonewalled, the more determined I became. I had been living the bachelor life for a number of years, partying with guy friends like a bunch of college fraternity boys, but had been feeling it was time for a change. My first sight of Crystal was like a skyrocket lighting my way to the future I wanted.

It took three months before Crystal finally agreed to go out with me. We married a few years later. With many friends, her modeling career, and interests of her own, she is completely accepting of my frenetic work schedule yet has actually induced me to take more time off for vacations, visits with her family and mine, and relaxing in the glorious Florida sunshine. I've never been happier.

CARVING A SLICE OF FAME

At the Philadelphia Home Show, about a month after we opened our doors, I discovered a man who had a product that sounded promising. A cherub of a gent, round of face and with a quick smile, he was a pitchman extraordinaire. I could see it from the first moments. He had maybe thirty people crowded around his booth watching him demonstrate a kitchen knife. They gawked as he sliced through pieces of shoe leather, a Coca-Cola can, even a car muffler and the head of a metal hammer. And then went on to show that the knife still wasn't the least bit dull by cutting tomatoes into thin, thin slices.

I remembered seeing these same knives months earlier, on a two-minute TV commercial. They were called the Ginsu knives, and I'm sure that name, sounding Japanese, added to the allure. But the knives were developed by an American and were manufactured in Freemont, Ohio.

The Ginsu knives were amazing, but nowhere near as amazing as the way the pitchman held that audience in the palm of his hand. I had the feeling I was watching a man born to his trade. Like the gypsies from all over Europe who gather in southern France every other year to elect a new king, I thought that if the pitchmen of the world were to gather to elect a king, this was the man they would choose.

I watched him go through his routine five or six times, and on each repetition he used exactly the same words. And each time he was done, something like half the people in his little audience reached for their wallets or purses and bought the product.

This was a eureka moment for me. I suddenly recognized that I could put this man in front of a camera, turn the camera on, let him do his pitch, slap an 800 number at the end, and have a show in the can practically ready to go on the air. What I envisioned in that instant would become the model for the classic infomercial, a model that in its basic form is still being used today.

Later on I would find out the whole story about this man, whose name was Arnold Morris. His talent wasn't some isolated fluke, like a kid from a dour family who turns into a great comedian. Arnold comes from an entire clan of pitchmen. His uncle Nathan had started the family tradition with kitchen products that he sold at county fairs, on boardwalks, and anywhere he could gather a crowd. Arnold had taken up the trade while still a youngster. Various cousins and other family members joined the business along the way, including an Arnold cousin who was the incomparable Ron Popiel. Ron liked to say about his generation of the family pitchmen that "my cousins could sell you an empty box."

I never saw Arnold try to sell an empty box, but on that first occasion, watching so many people pull out their money to buy his knives, my brain shifted into high gear. When I first started using half-hour television shows to generate leads for selling business franchises, it sure beat standing in a hotel meeting room doing a presentation in front of thirty or forty people. But even though the television exposure had started bringing many more leads, it was just a door opener. We didn't make any money until we had been through the whole process of convincing the guy, convincing the wife, convincing the bank, and finally getting his signature.

Selling products didn't have any delays like that, especially if you could use a pitchman like Arnold, conditioned to set up his little stand anywhere, gather a crowd, do his few minutes of pitch, and have people practically throwing their money at him—instant cash. The unbelievable part was that his buyers grew impatient for him to finish and take their money. They were so eager, it looked as if they wanted to interrupt him in midsentence and demand he take their dollars and hand them the product.

When Arnold finally took a break, I asked him, "How long have you been doing this?" He said, "Thirty years." He had started in the mid-1950s, sometimes working alongside a hulking guy named Ed McMahon, later known to millions for his nightly role on *The Tonight Show* in the Johnny Carson years, intoning the much-mimicked, "Heeeeeeere's . . . *Johnny!*" I figured, *This must be the best knife salesman in the history of the world.* The man was *that* good.

Instead of Arnold performing in front of little clusters of people, I could put him in front of millions.

Arnold had been buying his knives from a marketing firm that had purchased the rights from the Ginsu creator, a man named Ed Valenti. The secret lay in the surgical stainless steel he used, and the angle of the serrations. The marketing company had been selling the knives on television using the two-minute commercial I had seen, then sold the company to some other folks; whatever they may have done right or wrong, they ended up filing for bankruptcy. I managed to get a deal to buy in quantity directly from the manufacturer, Douglas Quikut, a division of the Scott Fetzer Company. (These days, the Fetzer company is owned by no less than Warren Buffett's Berkshire Hathaway.) But Quikut wouldn't allow me to use the "Ginsu" name, probably figuring that Quantum was just some upstart company they had never heard of, so they would be better to hold off for the time and allow the name to be used when a more established marketer came along.

We needed to come up with a different name, and Arnold suggested "The Blade." Okay, not very imaginative, but as things would turn out, it wasn't a name we would stay with very long.

We shot the show overnight at a location as unlikely as it was sensible: a New Jersey grocery store called King's Supermarket. "Sensible" because all the steaks, oysters, vegetables, canned goods, and other food products we needed for the show were already at hand. One of the store employees stayed on through the night to come up with any spur-of-the-moment items we might decide to use and to keep tally on the cost of everything that fell under Arnold's knives.

We arrived at the supermarket around closing time to start setting up. The arrangement was that we could have all the time we needed, up to a point: we had to leave the place as clean as we found it and be out of there by 5:00 in the morning so that the arriving workers could start getting ready for the first-of-the-day customers.

Tim and I did everything on the production except handle the camera and edit the footage. There wasn't any need for writing a script. On cue, the photographer just turned on the camera and our smooth-tongued pitchman launched into his finely honed spiel. Whatever I asked for, he could give me on the first try, polished to perfection. By the end of the night, we were calling him "One-Take Arnold."

The final production turned out to be a little more elaborate than I had first imagined. I set my staff to tracking down some of Arnold's satisfied customers. We selected a few and shot testimonials—butchers saying it was the greatest knife they had ever used, grandmothers in rocking chairs who had bought their knives from Arnold twenty-five years earlier proclaiming that it was still as sharp as the day they bought it.

We were already learning that direct-response television does better with a little tongue in cheek, which is what we had in mind when we labeled the show "Arnold's Gourmet Kitchen." Arnold was no gourmet chef, and his demonstration of slicing through hammers and automobile mufflers wasn't exactly what you expect to see a gourmet chef doing. I'm not sure that very many viewers consciously understood the joke, but that wasn't the point.

GOING GINSU!

As soon as we began to test market Arnold's show, it was obvious we had a big winner on our hands. Orders started pouring in from the very first day. A representative of the manufacturer was soon on the phone with me to say that the firm would now be happy to license the name "Ginsu" to me.

Our success meant that the notion of building an infomercial around a top-quality pitchman simply doing his pitch in front of the camera was an effective approach.

> In any highly competitive field, you have to be prepared to spring into action very quickly when a new product or approach comes along. He who hesitates gets the market stolen.

These professional pitchmen travel gypsylike from one show to another for about forty weeks a year. I immediately started hopping around the show circuit, roaming the floor, and looking for the guys good enough to talk people's money right out of their wallets. I signed up these pitchmen as fast as I could, knowing that if I didn't, the growing pack of competitors baying at our heels would read the meaning of the success our knife show was enjoying and start looking for available pitchmen they could build shows around.

I was happily successful in discovering the best of the pitchmen, producing the infomercials, and getting them on the air, one after another.

THE CASH-FLOW NIGHTMARE

The only hitch in the Ginsu deal was one that burdens the entire industry and that would come back to bite me in the ass repeatedly through the years. We had to pay for the product up front, in large enough quantities to be able to ship as the orders came in. Customers grow impatient quickly. If their product doesn't show up fairly soon after they've ordered it, many will call back and cancel or will return the product when it finally arrives. So you can't really wait until you have a few hundred customers lined up, then call the manufacturer and place your order. You need to have the product on hand or at least on its way to you when the infomercial airs.

We had already paid out one month's rent plus the security deposit for the office space. We had to cough up another large bundle for airtime. We were putting the money out before we got paid. Tim and I were dipping into the kitty for ourselves barely enough to keep body and soul together. In addition to the secretary (we had managed to find one willing to stay), we had taken on four salesmen who were out beating the bushes for our next big product, and even though they were working on commission only, we still had to cover their expenses.

It was a time for swimming as hard as we could to keep from sinking. I had met Arnold in August, made the deals in September, finished the show in October, and we had it on air in November. I was in the car of a business associate on the way to a meeting when I called our phone center for a report on the orders from the first airings. I shouted so loud that the driver almost veered into another car. I was hopping around in excitement: the numbers were unbelievable. We had hit a home run.

Just one problem: By then, we were dangerously low on cash. It was like an oil well coming in but you don't have any money left to cap the well and start pumping the oil. Still, I wasn't going to let the ugly cash picture spoil the excitement.

On the debit side, we were buying 1,000 knife sets at a time at $10 a set and spending $500 to $800 per half hour of airtime on twenty stations, plus the cost of the 800 number, a customer service outfit, and on top of all that, the bank was holding 5 percent of gross sales in reserve. But we were clearing $3 to $4 per knife set, which meant we were netting tens of thousands of dollars a month, which very quickly grew to *hundreds* of thousands.

That sounds like quite a respectable income for a start-up company a few months after going into business with its first product—using a sales technique never used before in this way, a technique so new that the descriptive term "infomercial" hadn't even been coined when we started. Impressions can be deceiving. Every spare dollar was going right back out the door to pay for more airtime and more knives. We had been very lucky that our first product was such a success. If sales continued to hold up, and there were no glitches, we would soon be able to start building some working capital.

Sometimes just when things are going well, the gods of business send a trial by fire to see how you will stand up. I received a call from the knife manufacturer to let me know that workers had walked out on strike from their plant in Ohio. The company was setting up a new factory in Arkansas. That doesn't happen overnight; it could only mean that our deliveries of knives would be held up for months. Customers began calling to cancel their orders. We had to pay our fulfillment center to hire extra people just to take the cancellation calls. Even so, some people were irate enough that they began finding out the phone number of our offices and calling us directly. Worse, some even wrote to their state attorney general to file a complaint.

It had made sense initially to charge the customer's credit card when the order was taken. Now I saw that that was part of our problem: most people would probably be patient about waiting for a product to show up, but not one they had already paid for. When you've paid, and the package isn't delivered pretty quickly to your front door, it's natural to wonder if the outfit is crooked and you've been cheated.

I changed the policy so that we would take the order but not put it through to the credit card company until we had the product in hand and were ready to ship. That cut down very significantly on the complaints, but it was scary, shattering, for the business. Not just because it was devastating to the cash flow, but it meant we'd have to cut our expectations. With dollars coming in later, we wouldn't be able to afford inventory and airtime at the same levels as before. We were simply going to be generating lower grosses.

A Gathering of Entrepreneurs

When I was starting out, being a young entrepreneur was not fashionable. Parents would ask, "When are you going to get a real job?" One person who noticed that there were young entrepreneurs everywhere who were struggling on their own to invent new ways of doing business was Verne Harnish, the head of a business consulting group. Verne set out to identify the top one hundred young entrepreneurs in the United States. Apple Computer, the hottest company in the world, doing $1.9 billion in annual sales, was the number-one company with an under-thirty head honcho. Microsoft, with a quarter billion in revenues, was number four on the list.

Verne sent out invitations for a conference that would bring together business students with as many of the young entrepreneurs as he could corral to attend the first session, in 1984, of what he was by then calling the Association for Collegiate Entrepreneurs. Two hundred assembled at MIT for the session. By two years later, attendance had blossomed to 1,100. Steve Jobs hadn't had time to attend while he was still at Apple; by this time he had been eased out the door and perhaps saw the invite as a vindication. He came and was showered with attention and lavished with well-deserved praise.

Verne was struck with the notion that the collegiate entrepreneurs now had a thriving organization to support them, but there wasn't any comparable group to connect the entrepreneurs on his top-100 under-thirty list with one another.

That inspiration, at the Friday night banquet in the ballroom of the Los Angeles Bonaventure Hotel, led Verne to start circulating through the room to spread the idea. I remember him coming up to me that night, his eyes burning with enthusiasm, and asking if I'd be willing to kick in $1,000 to be a founding member of the new group. I knew how much I had been learning all along from people like Neil Balter. I wrote Verne a check on the spot.

I had to laugh when I heard Verne's description of me in those days. He remembers me as "a cigar-smoking inferno of energy, a hyper-fast-talking ball of energy who everybody knew was wickedly smart." He also claims I was always the one leading the party. Verne got the idea that this was the only crowd I was comfortable hanging out with, because these other guys were about as hard-charging and success driven as me.

By a year later he had signed up twenty-two people for what was then called the Young Entrepreneurs Organization (YEO), later renamed the Entrepreneurs Organization (EO). The requirements were simple: you had to be under thirty, you had to be the head of a company grossing at least $1 million a year, and you had to recognize the value of learning from your peers.

When I had moved to the Philadelphia area a few years earlier, I traded a crowd of friends and an active social life for an eighty-hour workweek and no time for meeting people. So when Beryl Wolk introduced me to a man who had a single daughter about my age, I started seeing her. The father, Alan Fineman, owned a chain of very well-known wedding stores, which I think must have made him all the more eager to put on a wedding for his own Amy. After dating for a few months, I succumbed to convenience and asked her to marry me.

The wedding took place at the grand old Warwick Hotel in Philadelphia. By the time our only child, Brian, was born in 1988, it was already clear the marriage wasn't going to work. Amy didn't like being married to an entrepreneur who came home late and spent the evening studying catalogs and making business calls; she didn't like having a husband who went off on business trips to all parts of the world without her. "I'd rather be married to a truck driver who was home every night," she took to telling me often.

The friction was going to lead to an explosion. I suppose it was inevitable.

WALLY WOK

You can't let a business problem scare you so much that everything comes to a standstill.

By 1988, the situation at Quantum was continuing on its path of promising but problematic. One answer to the slowdown in deliveries of the knives would be discovering a new product that might have the same kind of sales potential. Two of the people from our small staff had continued that hunt at a housewares show at the Javits Center in Manhattan, and I decided to head over there myself to see what they were finding.

They both reported, "Nothing here. It's a waste of time." Not to take anything away from them, but my approach is different, maybe because I like people and connect well. Moving quickly around the floor, at each booth I'd find the guy in charge and tell him about our way of selling products with infomercials.

You have to start by explaining what you do and what you're looking for, before you can expect the other guy to offer you something that might be of interest. I'd say, "That's what I do. What do you have here that has a great story you could tell in a thirty-minute show?" The guy would look around his booth, where he had maybe five hundred or a thousand different items. He'd pick the two or three he thought might fit the bill.

At one booth, an engaging Englishman was offering kitchen knives. I thought, *If they're good enough, maybe we can sell these as a substitute until the Quikut people get up to speed again.*

The pitchman, who introduced himself as Wally, let me know that he was having as much of a problem with his supplier as we were with ours. But he said, "I've got another product I think you're really gonna love." He showed me a wok and told me it was "unbelievable." He said, "When you see what this does, you're going to be blown away." I said, "Wally, I'm not interested. A wok is a wok. Anybody who cares about wok cooking can buy one for ten bucks at Kmart."

He said, "No, Kevin, you don't understand. This one *does* have a story." I was willing to listen.

"This is a *hand-hammered* Chinese wok," he told me. "It's made the way they were doing it two thousand years ago in mainland China. They start with a wooden mold, lay out a flat piece of metal, and hammer on it about eight thousand times, shaping the metal sheet to the wooden mold."

He was building up steam as if he were doing a pitch to a crowd of potential customers. "The finished wok has a series of ridges on the inside," he said, pointing them out to me. "The ridges are what makes the cooking authentic, because when you're cooking Chinese food, the meats take a lot longer than the vegetables. So with this wok, you pull the vegetables up into the ridges where they cook a lot more slowly, while the meat or chicken cooks faster in the bottom of the pan directly over the heat."

Wally is giving me his demonstration while he's talking. He has a bamboo brush that he's using to clean up the wok between each batch of food, which he says is what they use in China the way we use a Brillo pad.

He had sold me, and I don't mean about buying one wok, I mean about producing an infomercial. Just as with Arnold and his knives, it wasn't only the product I was sold on but the sheer raw talent of the pitchman, which was irresistible. I could already see this as our next big product.

My brother thought I was crazy. His reaction was the same as mine had been at first: if you want a wok, you go out and buy one for a few bucks; you don't buy one from a television ad for $39, which is what we would have to charge for the set, with the wok, the brush, and a sheet of instructions. My whole staff tried to talk me out of this, insisting the product was so overpriced that we'd take a bath with it.

> Too often in life we let ourselves be governed by intellect when we should be trusting our instincts.

I've been guilty often enough myself of letting my intellect overrule my instinct. This time, though, I was smart enough to listen to my gut. We bought the rights to the product, signed up Wally to a long-term contract as the pitchman, and got set to produce the infomercial.

We had started getting our feet wet in the infomercial business with the same kind of thinking we'd grown used to selling franchises: the businessperson whose product we're selling pays in cash for the cost of production, up front. I talked to the man who actually owned the rights to the wok, a chap with the unlikely name of Max Ker-Seymor; Wally in fact worked for Max's company, Westminster. But he wouldn't go for the idea of fronting the $10,000 cost, so I financed the show myself and kept a bigger piece of the project.

We were just about to shoot a new version of the knife infomercial. I told Wally, "If you can come over on that day, I'll give you two hours in front of the camera to tape the wok show." This time around we could afford a studio instead of space in the back of a neighborhood supermarket. Wally came into the studio, we turned on the camera, and he did his pitch—eighteen minutes from start to finish. With the testimonials and the close-ups, it came out to the full twenty-eight minutes for filling a half-hour time slot on television.

Like Arnold, Wally had no problem with it. He did it in one take. The total production cost for the whole day, putting two shows in the can, was $8,500, and would prove to be a bargain.

Ker-Seymor had a deal with the manufacturer in China, so we had to buy the wok sets through him. It was a bottleneck: his line of credit wasn't big enough for buying more than ten thousand woks a month. To place an order, he would go to his bank and put up funds for a letter of credit for however many he needed, at $12 per unit. When the letter of credit reached the wok makers in China, they would present the paperwork to a functionary in a government office and receive a document enabling them to buy the steel plates. It could take a month or more for the workers to hammer enough woks to fill a sizeable order. When the order was finally ready, the woks would be loaded onto a ship for the weeks-long voyage to the United States.

I would have preferred to buy directly from the Chinese factory, but we couldn't afford the out-of-pocket cash over the three months from buying the letter of credit to having the product clear customs in the United States and be delivered to our fulfillment company's warehouse. I still had to pay when placing the order, but since we had a steady flow coming in, with this arrangement we had to put up the money only some three or four weeks in advance.

When the first 10,000 woks arrived, the man who owned the warehouse we were using in Long Beach, California, called with some very bad news. "I've got the ten thousand woks you ordered," he said. "Every one of the woks is covered with rust, and the brushes are rancid with a moldy coating." I asked, "Isn't the shipping company liable?" He asked if we had specified that the goods be stored in the ship's hold. No, we had just asked for the least expensive shipping. That turned out to mean the stuff had been strapped down on the open deck instead of being stored below decks, protected from the weather.

Some lessons you learn the hard way: We had never ordered a product from overseas before and didn't know enough to specify where it was to be carried while crossing the ocean.

It was like being hit in the head with a sledgehammer. On top of the $120,000 we had paid for the woks, we had laid out another $200,000 on media buys, the infomercials were already running, and our fulfillment company was sitting on $400,000 in orders. It had taken sixty days to make and deliver these woks. If we had to wait another sixty days for replacements, we would be out of business.

What do you do in a case like this? Cancel all the orders, write off the $320,000 already spent, and start all over? What would you have done?

If you thought of trying to scrub off the rust . . . give yourself a pat on the back. We set a couple of workers to the task of attacking a few of the woks with Brillo pads. Hard work, but the rust came off. With enough elbow grease, they actually regained the brilliance of the wok that Wally had first shown me. We hired a team of young, muscled guys to take on the daunting task of returning 10,000 steel woks to their original shine and purity. And we had another 10,000 brushes shipped by air; they cost us only twenty-five cents apiece.

Right from the start, the Great Wok of China joined the Ginsu knives as a spectacularly successful product.

I had originally begun using half-hour television commercials as a lead-generation device for my business/franchise sales operation. These stories of how that operation morphed into using the same basic approach for selling products holds a key lesson that I think can apply in almost any business:

Don't sell the product—sell the story.

One day I received a phone call from a man, a smooth-talking Russian named Ira Smolev, who was running a company called Synchronal. We had originally met a few years earlier when he wanted to buy some time from me out of the six hours a day I owned on the Discovery Channel. At the time he had offices in a residential high-rise building in New York, with his staff scattered among several different apartments. However, within minutes of discussion I could see and hear how sharp he was in business and how he held command of his company and employees despite physical appearances. He had an intense interest in learning what I was doing in business; he listened, studied me, took in the discussion, and made me an offer. I found out quickly that after doing business with Ira, I was going to make a lot of money.

Our money crunch was painful. The first batch of woks was beginning to ship but the time for scrubbing the rusted woks had thrown another monkey wrench into our money situation.

Instead of shipping as fast as the orders came in, we couldn't ship any faster than our muscle boys could turn out usable woks. The money wasn't arriving in the usual flood but in a trickle.

I thought I might be able to work out a deal with Smolev for help in rolling out the wok show. By then Synchronal had become the thousand-pound gorilla of the industry, now operating out of an office building in the heart of Manhattan, at Forty-fifth and Broadway, where the company occupied an entire floor—forty-five thousand square feet.

We agreed that Ira would license the wok show from me, put it on the air in markets I wasn't covering, and pay Quantum $6 for each wok they sold. He guaranteed us a minimum of $240,000 in royalties a month, with an added provision that the agreement would be voided if they failed to make the payments.

When I got back to Philly with the news, Tim and I were high-fiving each other and jumping around on desks. We now had absolutely no costs on this product, and no demands. Synchronal would be buying the media, taking the orders, financing the inventory, shipping the product, and handling the customer service. In an instant, we had gone from a successful but desperately cash-starved operation to a guaranteed income of $60,000 a week. *Sixty thousand a week!*

Once a month when that check arrived, it was like manna from heaven: $240,000, which would eventually total in the millions, on a show we had produced at a cost of less than two week's profits. Talk about a return on investment!

I called the bank one day to find out the balance, and it was over a million dollars. I was a millionaire.

THE BIG TIME

Successful businesspeople are problem solvers. I believe that's the first and most important requirement. You can do very well in business without a college degree, without a solid knowledge of accounting, without a good advertising sense. Some even make it without what's called "street smarts." Very few succeed without being good at coming up with ways around challenging situations that can't be found in the pages of textbooks.

We began 1988 as a thriving company with excellent income but still plagued by those unrelenting severe cash-flow problems. We were selling all the woks we could get, 2,500 a week. The delivery of the Ginsu knives was back on line, and we were moving 5,000 a week. In January and February we did about $2 million in sales, netting $20,000 to $25,000 weekly. I took $15,000 of that to buy all the airtime I could, pay the overhead, and spend everything left over on buying product. As soon as money came in, we would wire it off within hours to media buyers for TV time and to the manufacturer of the knives and the distributor of the woks.

I would have loved to be ordering 30,000 or 40,000 woks at a time. We could easily have sold that many, but we could only have gotten them by prepaying a letter of credit months in advance, which we still couldn't afford. Meanwhile I was nervous that someone else would come in with a competitive product and steal our market, selling to all the people we weren't yet reaching because we couldn't afford to buy the product in larger quantities. That's a really frustrating position to be in.

The China wok wasn't in the same class as our earlier products in terms of earning power, but still a product that would make any start-up company break open the champagne to celebrate. In just the first two years, the product brought us a profit of $3 million.

Though we certainly didn't recognize it at the time, with Wally and Arnold we were launching a tradition. We had offered Wally the choice of a flat $1,500 for appearing in the infomercial or fifty cents for every wok we sold. He gambled on the fifty cents. Good decision for him, a costly one for me. I put Arnold in front of mass audiences and sold millions of knife sets. Over time we paid him a million and a half dollars. Today, twenty years later, Arnold is still on television, and still using virtually the same words he was using so successfully when I first put him on the air.

In the years to come, we would make million-dollar and multimillion-dollar payouts to more than a hundred pitchmen like Wally and Arnold and folks who have found products for us, and we're still doing it.

Unfortunately, you can't always trust the people you're doing business with, as we were about to find out.

5

ON TOP OF THE WORLD

*I feel sorry for the person who can't
get genuinely excited about his work. . . .
He will never be satisfied.*

—Walter Chrysler

One day a man invited me to his home in Beverly Hills to see a product he called a Food Dehydrator. I was interested, but he insisted on terms that I couldn't agree to, and I turned him down.

I didn't think anything more about it until much later, when this same man, a master of self-promotion, gained note as one of America's premier pitchmen, on a par with the Ginsu knife's Arnold Morris. It was that cousin of Arnold's I mentioned earlier: Ron Popiel.

While I was turning out my first one hundred infomercials, Ron was carving a career as the master of the one-minute and two-minute spots.

Arnold tells a story about Popiel once becoming fed up with

a couple of guys trying to pitch a vegetable slicer. He took over the pitch, even though he had no idea how to operate the gadget, leading him to turn the vegetables into a soggy mass. Yet when he was done, his listeners, dazzled, reached for their pocketbooks. The unsuccessful pitchmen he had taken over from couldn't understand it. Arnold says that Popiel explained the secret: "I know how to ask for the money."

Strikeout

By early 1989, I barely had time to be surprised or pleased at how fast the company was growing. We had been in business for less than a year but had already been forced to staff up to handle the volume. In addition to the secretary, we now had a receptionist, a staff bookkeeper/accountant, and rooms full of temps who opened the mail, did the data entry for the thousands of checks pouring in, shipped product (at first), or sent reports off to our new fulfillment house (once the orders started being dumped at our office door faster than we could process them), and got the videotapes sent off to the cable stations in time to go on the air.

Our next product was discovered by Arnold Morris himself at the Chicago Housewares Show: a wickedly clever handheld kitchen gadget called the Daily Mixer that the exhibitor claimed could speed up the work of a cook (read "mom" or "dad") with chopping, mincing, blending, whipping, crushing, or grinding "virtually any food in almost any container." It could even make whipped cream out of skim milk in under a minute.

I cut a deal with the exhibitor in January, produced the show in February, had it running on cable stations in March, and in April we tallied $4.7 million in sales of the product. Before long the manufacturer was running his plant twenty-four hours a day, and we were taking the entire output, selling 15,000 to 20,000 units every week.

Over time, as the industry grew, we would all discover that the industry average is one home run out of every three times at bat. We had just about the same average as everybody else. One product that I thought was a sure thing, for example, was the shower-head designed to shut off automatically if the water got too hot. Maybe I was influenced by having grown up in a home where taking a shower carried a certain danger: someone only had to start the washing machine or even flush the toilet, and your water was suddenly scalding. When we started test marketing the infomercial, we thought our call center must have had a power failure—they reported only a trickle of orders. But it wasn't a power failure at the call center: the product was a complete disaster.

We took the failures in stride, knowing that the winners would keep us vastly profitable.

Growth Spurt with a Downside

The job of finding products was getting easier. The Quantum Marketing name appeared in the credits of each show; altogether the name was appearing on cable television thousands of times a week. All across the country, people with products to sell began calling us. And not just calling. Too many made the trip to Philly and lined up outside my door, without an appointment but with hopes and dreams, most of them cautiously guarding a cardboard box or other container hiding what they hoped would be their key to riches.

By the second quarter of 1989, I knew we were busy and growing at an unbelievable pace, but I hardly had time to dwell on the idea that we were making history.

When I got the financial report for the second quarter of 1989, I thought maybe there was some mistake. There wasn't. In those three months, we had sold $7.5 million worth of products and were throwing off profits at an annualized rate of about $5 million. The company had been in business for eighteen months. We had gone from zero to *wow*.

It's nearly impossible to grow that fast without dropping the ball now and then. Our faster-than-the-speed-of-sound growth rate was dazzling but came with a set of problems totally new to me. Overnight we had become a multimillion-dollar business. We were staffing up like crazy—five people, ten, fifteen, twenty . . . but they all still reported directly to me. My office was a merry-go-round, I was working twelve- to sixteen-hour days, and I was beginning to think that if I kept that up, I'd probably never see old age.

I still had my hand in everything—reviewing the show scripts, producing the shows, telling the editor what to use and where to cut, going to the trade shows, buying the media, keeping tabs on the people handling customer service, fulfillment, and ordering of inventory—which was never done until I had personally approved each order. In the office, I spent all day on the phone, in meetings, and looking at products brought in by people who stood outside my door. I was in constant motion. Pushing nine o'clock at night, I'd finally make it home—with a briefcase full of paperwork I had no time for reading during the day. But even the reading was in spurts because of the phone calls from people who knew they couldn't get me to focus if they caught me in the office. I'd turn in about 11:30 or so and be back at my desk by 8:00 the next morning.

We were making money like crazy but throwing some of it out the window—losing orders because the phone service couldn't handle the volume; losing orders while we switched over to a larger phone service; overlooking opportunities because I was personally too busy to follow up; missing important decisions because all decisions had to be approved by me; and experiencing costly mistakes by people who were hired but no one had the time to train.

We were also hampered by a hiring process that was less than ideal. Need a CPA? My wife's brother is available. Need someone to take over the ordering of inventory? Someone's cousin is looking for a job or some staff member knows a lady who could probably handle the work.

Not everybody has the stomach for contending with such a frantic environment. We had folks who would show up for three days and never come back.

I know now that there's such a thing as growing too rapidly.

Recruited

I received a phone call one day from YEO founder Verne Harnish. In conjunction with the business school at MIT and Bernie Goldberg, the publisher of *Inc.* magazine, Verne had created a program they were calling "The Birthing of Giants," designed to bring together for three days businesspeople he considered to be the most promising young entrepreneurs to learn from professors, successful entrepreneurs, and each other. Verne and his co-organizers wanted to create a case study of a young company that had grown very rapidly right out of the starting blocks. He explained what he was up to and asked about our revenues.

My answer was obviously what he was looking for. He asked if I'd be willing to let me and my company sit for our portrait as the basis for the case study. He was honest about warning me that my life and my company would be an open book. The effort would involve repeat visits by business professor Neil Churchill and his researchers, probably hours of interviews for me, ditto for any of my staff whose brain they wanted to pick. It would mean allowing him to pore through all my books and records. The only payment would be whatever recognition we might get from the business community.

He didn't say it, but I understood that the case study might tear us apart. Despite the company's success, I had never set foot inside a business-school classroom. Any analysis by learned professors and highly experienced management gurus would likely show that I was making huge mistakes. In a business where the cash lands in the bank account one day and goes right back out the door hours later—the risks of being shown up as a business dummy were huge.

Still, Verne can be very convincing. Despite the already impossible work pressure and demands on my time, I said yes.

GOING HOLLYWOOD

A schmoozer like me, always looking for the next product and anybody who might trigger my next marketing idea, is always eager to find time for a meet-and-greet function where the conversation flows as smoothly as the cocktails. On a trip to Los Angeles, I tagged along to a cocktail party at the Beverly Hills Hotel, where I fell into conversation with a heavy-set, jovial, dapper man who introduced himself as Earl Greenberg. He was a lawyer, he said, the vice president of Compliance and Practices for NBC, which he explained meant he was the head man for making sure that shows didn't contain any banned swear words, that sweaters and skirts covered appropriate areas, and the like. The network's Lord High Judge of Decency, in other words. Before that he had been executive producer of various network programs including Regis Philbin's morning show. He was a great teller of stories about movie and television stars, and a consummate LA flesh-pressing glad-hander.

But Earl didn't want to spend the rest of his life as a lawyer. He was looking for something "more challenging, more rewarding."

When I described our infomercial business and how fast we

were growing, Earl said, "I'm very intrigued by what you're doing. Look, you're producing television in a little place outside Philadelphia, and I'm based in the entertainment capital of the world. I could show you how to produce in a big way." *Great,* I thought. *Here's a man who might be able to take over producing our shows, and also help us grow even faster.*

Soon I was flying back to the West Coast again to attend a television trade conference with him. You couldn't help but be impressed—Earl seemed to know every executive and celebrity in the industry. Regis Philbin threw his arms around Earl. Joan Rivers ran up for a big hug. Vanna White fawned over him. I was starstruck. *This guy really is connected,* I thought. *He can open any door.*

Since then I've learned that people in Hollywood throw that kind of love-you-forever greeting on one another. It doesn't mean they really like you, trust you, or are willing to do a project with you.

But I was impressed by everything I knew about Earl, and I hired him. Not to work at the Quantum offices in Fort Washington, Pennsylvania, of course. We found office space on Camden Drive, in the heart of chic Beverly Hills 90210. Again I was lucky: just as with our first QMI quarters, the previous tenant had taken a hike in the middle of his lease, leaving behind furniture, plants, and pictures on the walls. For fifty cents on the dollar, I rented two thousand square feet of the space with an option on the rest of the six thousand square feet. It was so impressive that later on I actually heard people saying, "Where did these guys come from!?"

The highest-paid person on our staff in Pennsylvania at the time was probably making something like $75,000. I negotiated a deal with Earl for a salary of $300,000 for one year, renewable, figuring he was one hell of a salesman and had such experience in television production that he would be well worth it. I saw his salary not as an expense but as an investment.

COMPETITION

In a hot new industry, even the guy who starts out as the innovator and leader soon begins to feel the hounds nipping at his heels. You only stay in front by coming up with ideas your new competitors haven't thought of yet. We were still having products offered to us, but other people were snatching up some of the better ones.

Stop and think about this for a minute: If you were running some kind of sales operation right now and faced a challenge like this, what would you do?

The United States is arguably the most innovative nation in the history of the world. Sure, plenty of powerful ideas come from other parts of the globe, but in sheer innovative power, the United States remains unmatched.

Yet nobody in the infomercial world was looking for product ideas from overseas. In 1990, I boarded a flight that would take me to the Far East—Taiwan, Hong Kong, and mainland China. In advance, I had put out the word through the Far East product trade journals and sent information directly to manufacturers.

My message was: "Come find out how to get your products seen on American television." And I suggested they bring along their most sizzling products for me to consider.

Hundreds of people crowded into the hotel ballrooms and auditoriums for each session. A lot of the men looking around saw their competitors, which is why they had the products they wanted me to see hidden in a box or wrapper.

In a week, doing three or four shows a day, I probably looked at a couple of hundred products, ranging from the useless to the trivial to the impressive—to the gotta-have. Some twenty to twenty-five of those I made a deal on and put into development.

Whatever business you are in, never stop looking for the next hot deal.

While in Asia, I made it a point to detour way out into the countryside to visit the factory manufacturing our woks, only to discover that "factory" was a hilariously inappropriate description. The woks were being made in a crowded open space maybe twenty by thirty feet, with the eardrum-shattering clatter of thirty people simultaneously pounding on steel plates to make them into woks. No wonder it took so long for them to fill large orders.

FRIENDLY COMPETITOR

Another infomercial company had opened in Palm Desert, California, named after its two owners, Bill Guthy and Greg Renker. I found that out when I got a call one day from Renker. He said, "We've just started in the business. I understand you're one of the pioneers; I'd like to come and see you." He came in, and I showed him around, talking very openly about our operations. When we came to the room where the co-eds were transcribing the infomercials that Sam Catanese's setup was recording, Greg was fascinated, calling it "unbelievable."

At the end of the visit, he told me, "You've given me some ideas and insights. Taping the airwaves is brilliant." So far, so good. Then came the kicker. "I want to set up the same kind of operation—but there's a better way to do this. If you'll share all your overnights with me, I'll pay half your costs for the salaries and everything else that's part of this operation."

When I got to know Greg better, I discovered that he has a master's degree in picking people's brains. I've come to admire the talent.

But in my office that day, I simply told him, "I'll let you know." When I had cooled off, I thought it over. A week later I called him and agreed to share our overnights with him in exchange for his paying half the cost.

Greg and I ended up forging a relationship. We did two business deals together over the next couple of years, and we've been friends ever since—despite one of those deals turning out to be less than a huge success. That was a joint venture, called "QGR" for Quantum/

Guthy-Renker. Greg and I each put up half a million dollars to market products that our company had the rights to.

We had grandiose ideas for this business. Here we were, two leaders in an industry so new that everything fresh you did was groundbreaking. Greg and I were out to set a new gold standard.

This would have been fine except that both of us held on to all the products we were pretty sure would be bang-up successes and handed over to the joint venture . . . well, not dogs, exactly, but products we didn't have as much confidence in. Two of the ten products did well enough that QGR showed a bit of a profit, but the joint venture never soared, and didn't last very long.

The good news was that we didn't have any problems as partners.

A good partner is a man or woman who will sit down with you when there's a problem, listen to you carefully, explain his or her position, and work with you to resolve the situation, looking for common ground that will leave both of you satisfied by the solution. Lots of people don't have it in them to do that.

One weekend I was scanning the overnight logs of other people's infomercials and found an item that made my blood boil: it was a show selling the Wally Woks, our Great Wok of China product. This was a show done by someone else, touting the same woks under a different name, but featuring the same spokesman, Wally himself—mostly with the exact wording as in mine, the same pitch he had been honing and using for years.

I felt completely betrayed. What the hell was going on here? And who was behind it?

Ira Smolev, of course—the man who was paying us that $240,000 every month for handling the sales of the woks.

I phoned Max Ker-Seymor, who owned the rights to the woks, and asked him what was going on. I was giving Max a dollar of my take, which he was splitting with Wally. Max said, "Ira Smolev called me. He said, 'Kevin is giving you fifty cents a wok; I'll give you more,'" and proposed they shoot a new infomercial with Wally that they could then run and not have to pay me any money on the sales income. Apparently Max didn't see anything unethical about that.

From the beginnings of the industry, we had been flying by the seat of our pants. When we made a deal, we shook hands on it, and that was that. I think some people call this a cowboy contract—left over from the days when a rancher and a cowboy sealed a deal with a handshake because neither of them could read or write.

For us it wasn't a matter of reading and writing but a simple matter of trust. No written contract, no noncompete clause. I guess just about any businessperson in the world could have told me that wasn't professional and would eventually get me in trouble. You didn't need a degree from Harvard Business School to know that.

On the other hand, I did have a copyright on our show. Ira thought he had avoided that trap by bringing Wally into the studio and producing a new infomercial. But since Wally had repeated his standard pitch essentially verbatim, Ira's show infringed on my copyright.

Another guy in my position would have picked up his phone and called his lawyer. I'm more of a man-to-man type. I picked up the phone and called Ira instead.

We exchanged friendly greetings. "How're you doing?"

"Great, how's it going for you?"

Then I said, "There's a rumor you're shooting a new show with Wally."

He didn't figure I had already seen the show. "Where'd you hear a rumor like that?" he challenged, probably hoping that if he stonewalled, I might figure the "rumor" wasn't true and back down. He was trying to deny it when I had caught him with his pants down.

At that point, I started coming on stronger. "Let's stop playing games," I told him. "I have a copy of the show."

That didn't throw him. In fact, I sensed a glimmer of admiration showing through the tough-guy veneer. "You're pretty sharp," he said. "How'd you get a copy?"

Instead of answering, I told him, "We need to meet."

A few days later I was sitting in his office and was about to get a lesson in how Ira negotiated. He would make a deal, even one written on paper and signed by both parties—and then start looking for any way he could find to improve the terms in his favor. He was all about renegotiating as many times as possible.

In person, Ira is slow talking and real smooth. His opener was a conciliatory "What's the matter here?" And he tried to defend himself by saying, "It's a low-budget show; you didn't spend much money to shoot it."

I don't like being cheated. But I'm not greedy, and I won't

bring in the lawyers and the boxing gloves if it can possibly be avoided. "Let's work something out," I said.

When I walked out half an hour later, we were still in business together. Ira agreed to drop his show and continue using mine instead; I agreed to accept one dollar less per unit. Our net profit on the woks dropped from around $240,000 a month to around $200,000, but it was still money that came pouring in with no effort at all from us.

In business as in a marriage, any dispute that leads to bringing in the lawyers is likely to end with everyone worse off. The combatants on both sides are likely to take an emotional battering. Even the winner will probably feel wounded by the battle. The lawyers are the only ones guaranteed to leave the battlefield unscathed and better off.

Still, I had to recognize that I had been cowboying my deals with the pitchmen.

I would have to become more professional.

6

NEW WORLDS TO CONQUER

Even if you're on the right track,
you'll get run over if you just sit there.

—Will Rogers

When you're sitting on top of the world, you have a dangerous inclination to feel as if nothing can go wrong. Your vision narrows to a focus that only sees sunny days and balmy breezes. That's how I was seeing my business in 1989.

Of course, Mark Twain once cautioned about the meteorological conditions in New England, "If you don't like the weather, just wait a few minutes." There would be storms ahead for us, but not before the company's life became vastly better. I had left Franchise America with my soul intact, bowing out with no bitter accusations, recriminations, or lawsuits over all the money that should have been going into my own pocket but landed elsewhere instead. The new company I had started with my brother Tim, Quantum Marketing Inc., was bounding along handsomely. We were already selling the Ginsu knives, the hand-hammered Great Wok of China, and the Daily Mixer. Our $5 million a year in profits was counterbalanced by the somewhat peculiar, cash-hungry industry we had been there at the creation of; we were plowing our earnings back into building the company, so money continued going out almost as fast as it was coming in.

Even when we seemed to be getting ahead, it was sometimes an illusion. My accountant alerted me one day about some income taxes that were due. I had incorporated as a Subchapter S business, meaning that profits flowed through to me as the sole owner, and I paid taxes on those profits as personal income. Just when I thought I was building up a nest egg, the accountant had some unwelcome news. I thought what I heard him say was, "I've finished doing your personal income taxes, and I'm afraid you owe the government $1.7 million."

I knew I hadn't heard him right. But that turned out to be exactly what he had said. I told him what I had always said in the past in situations like this: "Go back, take another look, and find out where the mistake is." He told me had been over the figures repeatedly, and there was no mistake.

I was in a state of shock. And worse was yet to come. "When is it due?" I asked. He said, "You'll have to pay it today if you want to avoid stiff penalties and interest." *Today!* I was devastated—and really angry to be given this bad news at the very last possible moment. To this day I don't know whether he didn't do the return until the very last minute or had known what I owed but couldn't face me with the unpleasantness until he couldn't put it off any longer.

My chief financial officer responded to my urgent call over the intercom and joined us. His answer to my inquiry about how much cash I had in the bank: "1.85 million." Unhappily, I wrote out a check to the Internal Revenue Service for $1.7 million—so much for building up a nest egg. Though on paper we were making $5 million profit a year, we now had a meager $150,000 to stay in business with.

Even today, the situation seems ridiculous. You work your tail off, figuring it's all worth the effort because you're racking up a hansome profit . . . and then discover you have to pay your "profit" out in taxes.

When that IRS check cleared the bank and came back to me, I carried it in my wallet for years, a testament to our rapid success and our misery-making lack of cash reserves—not to mention painful evidence about how unsophisticated I was. Occasionally some skeptic would hear the story and think I had to be exaggerating, and I would pull out that check, with a combination of pride and secret embarrassment.

The profits being generated by the Ginsu knives infomercial and the others that followed spawned a pack of hungry imitators. As the field became more crowded, finding the next hot product was becoming harder and harder. Too many others were haunting the trade shows and scouring the catalogs. "I've already made a deal with so-and-so" became a phrase that my salespeople were hearing far too often.

And the business was becoming competitive in other ways, too. For example, we had owned a six-hour-a-day block of time on the Discovery Channel. When the renewal came up, we found we had been outbid and had lost that valuable slot.

Sometimes in a situation like this, there's little you can do except work harder than the other guys and offer better deals. Naturally that just makes the cost of doing business go up and up. And then an idea struck me one day. I was a regular reader of *Variety.* (I believe as an entrepreneur that reading trade publications, even in fields totally unrelated to your own, can sometimes give you an incredibly valuable angle on something that applies to your world. Even though I subscribe to a pile of journals in diverse fields, still, to this day, I'll drop into a Barnes & Noble and spend two or three hours going through stacks of magazines and new publications, looking for ideas and products.)

The *Rambo* movies were very popular at that time. I enjoyed them as a moviegoer, and I enjoyed the thought of all the profits the pictures were making for the producers. From *Variety,* the names of the *Rambo* producers were familiar to me—Golan and Globus—and I had read that their profits weren't just coming from the domestic box office. *Rambo III*, released the preceding year, brought in $53 million from showings in the United States and $135 million from around the world.

Golan and Globus, big-time movie producers, were raking in money from all over the globe. I was a big-time infomercial producer. Why couldn't I follow in their footsteps?

At that point, Tim and I had a library of about sixty infomercials. Maybe what was so good for *Rambo* could be just as good for the Harringtons.

In a burgeoning industry, market conditions can change with alarming suddenness; when competitors start crowding in, it's time to look for opportunities no one else has spotted yet.

I eagerly laid out my thinking to the rest of the Quantum staff: we should start figuring out how to launch operations globally before anybody else in our increasingly crowded industry thought of doing it. Instead of the response I expected, it was as if I had just broken wind in public. I got a variety of pained expressions, together with comments like, "We don't know anything about doing business overseas," and "We've got all these great contacts in the United States and none anywhere else," and "Focus, focus—we need to keep our focus!"

I hadn't built a multimillion-dollar business by getting discouraged when other people rained on my parade. And as far as I could see, going overseas had to be a great way of leveraging existing assets. Maybe it would turn out that there were some compelling reasons why the idea wouldn't work, but I sure wasn't about to give up without trying.

I just had to take a shot at it. I had to see whether the Ginsu knife could do a Rambo overseas, because if it could, then every show in our library held the prospect of generating revenues ranging from excellent to beyond fantastic. Creating foreign versions couldn't be all that difficult and certainly not very expensive: I could translate a $200,000 production into another language for probably on the order of a couple of thousand dollars. And there had to be seventy or eighty foreign countries where there were enough people with disposable income to make infomercials worthwhile. Just thinking about it was enough to bring a smile. I was hell-bent on making it happen.

Except that I didn't quite know how to get started.

On the other hand, *where* to get started was a no-brainer. Where else but England? We had been buying a lot of time on Lifetime Television and somewhere I had read about a similar operation in England—the Lifestyle channel for women. A little research showed that Lifestyle was owned by a British company called WH Smith. They also owned a companion channel, Screensport, which was the ESPN of England.

Why does it have to be so difficult to get through to the right person in a company where you don't have any contacts? I kept calling WH Smith, leaving a message for somebody who sounded as though he or she might have the appropriate job title, then making follow-up calls when I didn't hear back, finally getting hold of the person only to learn that it not only wasn't the right person to talk to, but he or she didn't know who was.

Knocking on a series of wrong doors can be frustrating, but if you're paying attention, it can also lead to valuable insights.

Eventually I picked up a crucial, almost unbelievable piece of information. The Lifestyle and Screensport channels went off the air at six o'clock every night. I almost dropped through the floor when I heard that. Why so early? Well, because that's when the old lady of British broadcasting, the government-owned BBC, went on the air with its evening news broadcast. And apparently nobody in his right mind would ever suppose that any English viewer would tune in to another program while the BBC evening news was on.

Undaunted, I kept on with my hunt for the person in charge of Lifestyle. I was used to the challenge of getting media people who had never heard of us to call back. But there was a lot more at stake here than just trying to get our shows on one more American cable television channel.

It took more than a month before I finally got through to the right person, a chap by the name of Peter Brice. I was elated. Yet I knew I better not blow this opportunity. There was only one way to test the international waters without the problems of translating into a language I didn't even know: the WH Smith channels were my only opportunity. And Peter Brice was the man guarding the door.

I started out by telling him I wanted to discuss buying the channel's off-air hours for my programming. I said, "I've been running on Lifetime in the U.S. for a number of years. If you need a reference, you can just call them." And I told him, "I want to come over and show you what we do and find a way that you and I can do business together."

He said, "Look, we only have four channels over here. BBC1 and BBC2 are owned by the government and run no commercials at all. The other two are showing thirty-second and sixty-second adverts, but under no circumstances would they show a half-hour commercial."

I didn't like the direction this was taking. He went on, "Now WH Smith has opened two satellite channels, and we're also showing a few adverts. But thirty-minute advertising shows? Forget it. 'Infomercial' is a foreign word to us. We have no interest in running infomercials."

In the United States, I had been dealing almost entirely with ad sales people. Now for the first time I was talking with a top-level guy. That didn't keep me from feeling extremely confident. Okay, maybe even a little cocky, because that's me. I just wasn't prepared to take no for an answer. I said, "Peter, you guys are dark. What difference will it make if I take some of your time when you shut down? It's found money for you."

He told me, "Our customer is not the American customer. Your half-hour adverts will offend our viewers. It will never work here."

After more back and forth like this, I had to accept that I wasn't going to sell him on the telephone. Without a word of truth in it, I said, "I'm going to be in England anyway," and argued that it would be worthwhile for him to give me thirty minutes. He said, "You'll be wasting your time," but finally agreed. I hung up, the air gone out of me over his stern resistance.

To England

My preparations for the trip involved nothing elaborate. I'm a great ad libber. No script, no elaborate notes, no rehearsals. I can walk in armed with samples of our shows, printouts of our earnings, press clippings, and letters of reference establishing me as a credible businessman, and expect to walk away with an agreement in principle for doing a deal.

I flew to London two weeks later, accompanied by Bobby Foster, the manufacturer of the Daily Mixer, who had a vested interest in the outcome since he made a $7 royalty on every mixer sold and was already calculating what his take might be if I could open up overseas markets. He had asked if he could come along, and I was frankly glad to have a companion. We landed on a typical British winter day—overcast, gray, and bitter cold. The emotional climate, though, seemed a good deal better.

My only previous overseas trip had been the one to the Orient, where I had found the people not exactly bubbling over with warmth and friendship. But here all of my initial contacts, from the Immigrations people to the cabdriver who drove us to the London Hilton, seemed courteous and genuinely pleased to have us in their country. What I hadn't anticipated was the cost of everything—at least double the prices at home. And the hotel room, also twice the price I was used to paying at home, turned out to be tiny, a real squeeze for two people, and heated by one of those old-fashioned radiators that had, even then, all but disappeared from homes in America and are certainly never to be found in first-class hotels on this side of the Atlantic.

Not yet a sophisticated traveler, I didn't know that with a little tactful persuasion I could probably have convinced the front desk manager to upgrade me to a more modern suite for the same price.

⌐ For the business session, I dressed buttoned-down, not just because I was meeting with a British executive but because by then it had become my style. I still looked younger than my age (at the time I was thirty-two but was often mistaken for my early twenties), and was still relying on the suit-and-tie getups to make me look a little more like someone to be taken seriously. Except perhaps in high-tech and any other go-go industry of the moment, for any younger man in business, dressing in suit and tie—especially when the suit is obviously expensive—helps build the aura of an established, successful executive. ⌐

Besides dressing conservatively, I had also started smoking large cigars for the same reason. They provided me a topic of conversation with like-minded executives, though I'm not sure they did me any actual good beyond the unqualified satisfaction a good cigar bestows—despite dirty looks from some non-smokers.

Bobby and I walked from the hotel to the Lifestyle offices in the Soho district, an area once known as a hangout for punkers with spiky orange hair but which had apparently morphed into a location for antique shops, expense-account restaurants, and the quite unimpressive buildings that nonetheless had signs indicating they housed the London offices of Disney, MGM, and other familiar movie companies.

Churchill was only half right with his line about the United States and England as two countries separated by a common language. Apparently we were also two countries separated by different ideas of doing business. At the Lifestyle building, we were shown not to Brice's office but to a small, cramped, nondescript conference room. Brice came in, a sandy-haired man with a mustache and a formal bearing. Despite my dressing to look older, he, too, seemed taken aback at the first impression that he was sitting down to do business with a kid. An *upstart* American kid, I imagine he might have been thinking. He offered a cordial but distant greeting. I got the impression of a rather cynical British stuffed shirt looking down his nose at me, a man who at that point didn't really give a damn about me or what I had to say. But I had come a long way, and I counted on the strength of my personality and the art of rapport I had honed in dozens of meetings like this to carry me through.

I ran the demo reel I had brought, made up of pieces from our infomercials on the hand-hammered wok and some of the others. His face started to light up as he watched the shows. I began to sense that I was going to be able to bring him around. When I showed him reports on the business we were doing, he asked perceptive questions. This was no dummy—he was sharp, with a keen perception for the finer points of a spreadsheet, and he was enthusiastic. To use one of my favorite expressions, he was blown away by the revenues we were generating and by the quality of the shows.

I had asked for half an hour of his time. He wasn't even looking at his watch. The half-hour time slot came to an end, and he was still asking questions. Better and better.

Then he said, "Kevin, I like what you're doing, but it will never work here. The British television viewer who has never seen more than a sixty-second television advert would be offended by your half-hour commercials. Our *entire audience* would be offended." I was almost knocked out of my chair. He'd been so impressed by the numbers and by the shows, yet here he was now telling me, "No way."

It was as if he was laughing me out of his office. His attitude was, "Go home, Yankee. Your ideas are not welcome here."

In a moment he was standing up, ready to say good-bye and leave a secretary to watch us pack up and see us out. He had stayed with me for nearly an hour, but I had never gotten to tell him the deal I was prepared to offer. He never gave me a chance to say how much income his company stood to make for his unused airtime.

When you have a deal that's not just good for you but good for the other guy as well—never let the door close.

Before he could leave, I said, "Now that I understand your culture, I'll do some more research and get back to you." He said he'd be open to that. Maybe he was just being polite. It didn't matter; I was counting on his answer meaning that he would take another call from me and allow me to come back. Maybe I could still turn his no into a yes.

But that might prove to be a pretty big maybe. All in all, the trip was going to cost me $6,000 to $7,000, and I might have nothing to show for it, and no easy test market for going international. For the second time, Peter Brice had left me feeling deflated.

PEOPLE WATCHING

I had a couple of other items on my agenda before returning to the States. Understanding people is a cornerstone of the infomercial business, and I have this unflagging curiosity about people of all kinds. Maybe that started as a result of my getting into this business, or maybe I got into the business because it was an outlet for whatever wisdom I had gathered about the way people think and respond. But I knew I wasn't going to be in England without getting a taste of the country and the people, and that was the first item on my agenda. My companion, Bobby, who had been to England before, dragged me off to visit Harrods, the best-known of the British department stores. I was struck by the formality of the place: a uniformed greeter wearing white gloves swung the door open for us as we approached. I was even more struck by the prices. After my initial experiences I shouldn't have been surprised, but everything seemed outrageously expensive.

Enjoying the view from the upper level of a double-decker bus, I wondered whether there is some defining character distinction between the people who sit on the lower deck and those who sit on the upper. And whether there would be a difference from one group to the other about buying products from infomercials.

I wanted to take part in the very British ritual of afternoon tea. One of the best places to observe Londoners going about this curious practice, according to the concierge at the Hilton, was at the famous Ritz Hotel—so very upper class, don't you know, that *ritzy* has entered the language as a word for swanky and glamorous. But our way in was barred by a maître d', who announced, "Gentleman wearing jeans are not permitted in the dining room." I guess another meaning for *ritzy* is "snooty."

Yet my money was good at the Mecca for cigar lovers, the esteemed Davidoff, where I treated myself to a $750 box of Cuban cigars while offering up a small prayer that they would not be seized by customs. I had a dinner of the traditional dish called shepherd's pie (like a meat pie, except the crust is made of mashed potatoes), and we spent the evening in a pub. I ordered a beer, and when it came, I sent it back because they had poured me a bottle that wasn't cold yet. Bobby laughed and clued me in that on our side of the Atlantic we drink our beer cold, and on their side they drink it warm.

Quest for a Studio

Ever the optimist, the second item on my agenda before returning home was a visit to Glasgow, where I had located a cable operator who had a studio and production facilities. En route there, I couldn't help noticing that the people living in the charming villages of the British countryside had little more shopping opportunity than the local greengrocer, butcher, chemist's (pharmacy), and hardware store. No Kmarts, no Wal-Marts, no big-box stores. I could just picture a nation of people starved for the kind of products we offer.

The cable operator was a man named David MacLachlan. (Okay, that wasn't really his name; I confess I don't remember it any longer, so that's the name I'll use.) I didn't see in him much

of the reserve that the Scottish people supposedly share as a leading characteristic. We spent a full day together talking about what
I would be looking for if I could manage to break down the resistance at WH Smith. He seemed to be genuinely enthusiastic
about the idea of my using his facility, and I came away thinking
that we wouldn't have much trouble arriving at agreeable terms.
Anyway, that was my impression, though the Scottish accent can
be damnably hard to understand for anybody not used to that
lilting inflection and those oddly pronounced vowels.

TRYING AGAIN

The following month I laid plans for a trip back to London,
where I would go with renewed confidence, this time with an
ace up my sleeve. In the United States, the cable operators told
us they hated our programs, hated the idea of running our
shows over their networks, but the money was too good to turn
down. We used to joke that infomercials were almost like a drug
to the station people: once they ran a few of our shows, they
were hooked—they couldn't get off it because the shows
brought in so much money without their having to lift a finger.
I planned to use the same strategy on Peter Brice.

Sure, not every cable channel in the United States was an easy
sale. Ted Turner said, "We don't want your shows. We won't run
them." (That's still true of CNN, but even for Turner the temp-
tation of the easy money would eventually prove too great, and
he began accepting infomercials on his TBS channel.)

Under a Microscope

Professor Neil Churchill and his researchers showed up to begin their work for the case study. To me, Neil was a typical college professor in his sweater and tie and with graying hair—the type of man you expect to see smoking a pipe. The graduate students with him seemed a little mesmerized at being on the inside of our entrepreneurial explosion; they found themselves witnessing the growth, experiencing the problems, even sharing in the high fives over the home-run shows.

Their first visit lasted ten days. The follow-up visits, phone calls, and requests for financial reports and other data stretched out for months. They would not tell me anything about what mistakes of mine they were discovering. Fortunately, I continued to be too busy to worry about it.

Forming a Plan

Still troubled over my turndown by Brice, I woke up in the wee hours one night with what I thought was a brilliant idea, one certain to overcome the determined reluctance I had encountered on my first visit. Possibly I should be giving Peter Brice credit for this; I still don't know to this day whether the idea was triggered by something he had said to me in our meeting or if it was original.

I knew from all my experience in the business that the programming departments hated us. I had developed a countermeasure: *sidestep the people most likely to say no and find others in the company to talk to.* In this case, that meant getting in to see the financial people. Even better were the salespeople: when a guy spends his days selling one-minute spots, and I come in and say I want to buy a strip of half-hour slots—the same time every night for the next three months—I have his attention. He's going to bring in a big chunk of business for his station or channel, and get a whopping big commission for himself, all with very little effort.

So I was used to giving my pitch in financial terms, which I had missed out on in my first session with Brice. But his resistance was so strong that I figured just a pounds-and-shillings presentation wasn't going to do it. How could I present a story that would light his fire? It was the answer to this question that woke me up in the middle of the night.

WH Smith was new to television, but they were already a well-established company, and the core of their business was in newsstands, thousands of them, all around the world. Probably you've never noticed the name, but you see lots of their newsstands in airport terminals and elsewhere. The typical one is all of about a hundred square feet. The key data was right in the company's annual report: the company's annual average profit per newsstand came to a value in British pounds that translated to roughly 37,000 U.S. dollars.

I decided on the figure I could guarantee I would pay the company for use of their dead airtime: a minimum of $500,000 a month, $6 million a year. From our years of experience in the

United States, I guessed we could sell enough product in England to generate that much commission for them. If I was wrong—if the Brits really hated the whole idea and changed the channel as soon as our shows came on—we could be out the entire first month's guarantee plus all the production expenses. But the potential of opening up the global market was simply too strong a pull. Call it a weakness on my part. Call it whatever you want. This was just something I *had* to try.

When I met with Brice again, I went prepared. Together we worked out the calculation: to bring in $6 million a year from their newsstand business, they would have to open an additional 162 newsstands.

Searching out suitable locations, contracting for the space, building the stand, hiring clerks who could be trusted to handle cash with no one looking over their shoulders—all that has to add up to a significant cost for every new installation. I said, "What I'm offering you is money you don't have to put out any effort for. You guys owe it to yourselves to test this. You owe it to your shareholders. Without any upfront costs, you'll get a check from me every month."

And I said, "If the content does turn out to be objectionable to your viewers, and you're getting nasty letters that say, 'Stop running those American ads,' you can simply take our shows off the air at any time."

The next little bit was the piece that had come to me in the middle of the night. Today the phrase is, "Show me the money!" I had realized *that's exactly what can work in a situation like this:*

show him the money. I pulled out a blank business check and right there in front of him, I made it out: Payable to WH Smith, $500,000. I left it undated but put my signature on it, and told him: "Hang on to this. After our first thirty days on the air, I'll put a date on it, and you can take it to the bank, toward your share of the first month's payment."

Brice was giving in. That check had a lot to do with it: half a million dollars; the five and all those zeros, and the prospect for another one for at least that much, *every month.* He said he would take the proposal to their board and be back in touch.

I heard from him only a few days later. Did my offer really go before the corporate board? Or did Brice just sit down with his boss and make the decision between them? I didn't care. All I cared about was the outcome: I had been given a green light.

Still, Brice was nervous. He was afraid there was going to be a huge backlash against his company. He said the initial deal would be only for thirty days, and my offer of a provision that they could take the shows off at any time, even during those first thirty days, would have to be written into the contract. The possibility of massive negative publicity was haunting him so badly that he even fantasized about a call from Buckingham Palace that the Queen had been offended. He was afraid his whole career might be on the line.

But when it came to the question of whether the Queen might object to our shows, I had an ace in the hole—once again the result of sheer happenstance almost too good to believe. As a consultant to oversee our shows and make sure they would be suitable to the British audience and not in any way inappropriate (remember when the Chevrolet Nova was marketed in Latin America under the same name, nobody having recognized in advance that in Spanish *no va* means *doesn't go*?), I had hired a retired British cop, a "bobby." As it turned out, his daughter worked as an assistant to the Queen, opening her mail. That didn't mean I would be able to sidetrack any royal displeasure, but at least I had a line inside Buckingham Palace if I needed one.

GEARING UP

Peter Brice was sitting on that half-million-dollar check of mine. The money to cover it had to come from our sales in the first thirty days we were on the air. I normally move fast; now I was going at hyperspeed. I was frantically driven to know whether this was going to be my most humiliating fiasco or the doorway to riches. Within three weeks I had hired a phone fulfillment center, decided on the products that would launch our introduction to the British people, and made deals with the talent for those shows. By week four I was in Glasgow starting to tape our first infomercial to air on the Lifestyle channel.

The Ginsu knife sets had been such a runaway success at home that it was as easy a choice as beginning our overseas efforts in England. Fortunately, Arnold Morris, the incomparable pitchman who had been such a major part of its success—and who had been my own springboard to more or less inventing the infomercial—was available and willing to come to frigid

Scotland for the shoot. The pitch was the same one he had been doing for so long (who would dream of tampering with success like that?). I had Arnold dress up in a traditional Scottish kilt. After the shoot, when we got to the editing suite, I fleshed out the soundtrack with popular British music of the day.

I had been paying attention when the WH Smith people had first seen samples of our shows and complained that they were "too hard a sell, too American."

"We'll reshoot them here," I had promised, and that's what we did. I had already located that fully equipped studio in Glasgow, where the technical skills were high and the costs more reasonable than in London. We did the studio scenes on the stage in Glasgow, where the consultant I had hired kept us straight on things like calling the stove a "cooker." For the voice-overs, of course, we used a British actor and fleshed out the shows with testimonials from enthusiastic British users of the knives.

Arnold's everyday enthusiasm rose to a pitch when he, I, our director, and a full camera crew clambered onto a double-decker bus for local-color exteriors. Used to the attention of hardly more than a dozen people at a time, Arnold seemed tickled by the stares of all the other bus passengers wondering who the celebrity was. Even funnier were the scenes of Arnold trying to look comfortable when surrounded by a troop of bagpipe players assailing his ears with their mournful sounds.

My local representative, the retired bobby, went to all important meetings with me, especially meetings at government agencies, flashing me subtle signals when my sometimes abrupt style was in danger of ruffling feathers. Having him in these meetings was a blessing, since so many of the people I had to engage with really didn't want to be talking to this pushy Yank with his crazy ideas about half-hour commercials. My emotional response from being polite and reasonable with people who don't want to be helpful ranges from frustration to being infuriated. In a situation like that, having someone along who can quietly throw a bucket of water at you now and then to cool you down is virtually an essential.

The other two shows I produced in new versions for the British introduction were the hand-hammered wok and the Daily Mixer. The team I had assembled did all of this, having three complete half-hour shows in the can and ready for airing in less than a month.

ON THE AIR

Our first show went on the air at 6:00 PM on April 12, 1990. There had been no fanfare, no TV spots or newspaper ads, for fear of an outcry in advance that might have led to a cancellation before the public had even a single chance to view the production and hear about those incredible knives.

The response was unbelievable. I had fantasized that the Britons might be enthralled by a convenient, reasonably priced product that they couldn't get in any local shop, but I couldn't even begin to guess how overwhelmingly they would glom on to the idea of buying from an infomercial. They took to it like an addict takes to his drug. As soon as the toll-free number flashed on the screen, calls began flooding in.

From the early days of this business, I had always calculated a target number for sales of a new product in the first hour after the first show aired, a number reflecting the sales we would need in order to break even; if we made that number, then experience had shown the follow-on sales the next day would bring in enough additional money to give us a profit. An hour after the first Ginsu knife infomercial aired in Britain, we had not made our magic number—we had made two-and-a-half times the number. I was elated, floating.

At the end of the first month, adding a date to the check Peter Brice was holding and letting him deposit it was no problem. We had received 50 percent more orders per 10,000 viewers than we ever received in the United States. Our new London bank account at Lloyds was flush with funds.

Nobody called in or wrote to complain; no newspaper critic or magazine columnist sounded any alarm. Peter Brice's fears about an irate message from some Buckingham Palace functionary, Lord Somebody-or-other communicating on behalf of Her Majesty the Queen, proved unfounded.

We did get mail, though. People began writing in to say how much they enjoyed our shows. Incredible!

The staff at the call center had been trained to say after taking a customer's order, "Thank you for your purchase. I'd like to tell you about a special I am able to offer you. I can sell you a second set at a 30 percent discount." Many of the callers would respond with something like, "Oh, would you? That is so kind," and place an additional order. They were grateful for the opportunity to buy the product, and we started to get reports that people were ending their call by saying to the person taking the order, "Tell Arnold we enjoyed him so much."

I signed a contract for all of the downtime on both of the WH Smith television channels for the next five years.

When the British equivalent of the Nielsen ratings came in, I was absolutely floored. Our wok infomercial was the second most popular show of any program on the Lifestyle and Screensport channels. Of the top-ten shows on those channels, three of them were our infomercials, and around Britain, fan clubs were forming for our pitchmen. Fan clubs!

The response generated one of the most unbelievable feelings I've ever had. I broke out the champagne, and my whole London team celebrated with backslapping and hugs and shouts of excitement. We had proved that the infomercial was more than just a tool for selling to the American audience. I experienced a sense of accomplishment greater than anything I had known. I knew I was going to be a person who would pioneer the infomercial around the world.

My experience with WH Smith taught me a lesson that has guided me many times ever since:

"No" doesn't necessarily mean "never." Sometimes it means, "You haven't offered me something irresistible. You haven't offered me something I can't afford to turn down."

"We Pay You"

Shortly after the first British infomercial aired, I boarded a flight to Cannes, France, for an industry conference called MIPCOM. They describe themselves as the global content event for buying, selling, and arranging the financing for films, television shows, and other digital entertainment. Held every year two weeks before the Cannes Film Festival, MIPCOM is where *Baywatch* became the biggest-selling TV show in history. You get the impression that every TV station in the world is there.

For a schmoozer like me, these conferences have always been a great place to socialize, pitch, and make contacts. I'm blessed with having very few qualms about introducing myself to complete strangers, even prominent people who are way more successful than me and celebrities other people might simply gawk at.

The station people were there to buy shows, mostly programming from the United States, paying a licensing fee to the producer for each episode they aired. They had come to spend money. My approach was a twist that caught them off guard.

I had a big sign on my booth that said, "We pay you to run our programs. Stop here to learn how." The sign was a grabber, even better than having a girl in a bikini manning the booth. People saw the sign and stopped, trying to figure out what it could mean. Whenever someone stopped, we would hand him or her a videocassette of clips from shows we had developed— cooking shows, exercise/fitness shows, and so on. Each cassette had a one-dollar bill attached. "We're paying you to watch this cassette," we'd tell them, "because *we're* going to pay *you* to air our shows."

People were baffled. "Everybody else is charging us for programming, and you're going to *pay* us?" they'd ask. "What's the catch?"

"At the end of the show, we run a toll-free telephone number, and people call in to buy a product. We pay you to air the show during your dead time at night."

That twist turned out to be a powerful door-opener.

By the time I got back to England, we had hired a few staff people to begin building the organization we would need to handle our British sales, which were increasing steadily. So it was a shock one day to be told, "We're losing a lot of business. Lots of people are hanging up."

"What's going on?"

"The people at the call center we hired can only speak English."

"But why is that a problem?"

"Somebody calls and tries to place an order in Spanish or German or Swedish, and when the clerk doesn't understand them, they hang up."

"Wait a minute," I said. "Do you mean there are that many people in England who can't speak any English?"

"No, no. We're getting calls from all over Europe."

"How can that be? We're only broadcasting in England."

"This isn't cable TV like in the United States. It's a satellite feed. People in fifteen other countries are discovering the show and calling in."

Fantastic, but my head was swimming. We had to find a way of selling to all the rest of Europe. Overnight, if possible.

And if it worked in Europe, where half-hour television advertising was entirely unknown, I couldn't see any reason why it shouldn't work in Japan, Latin America, the Middle East—anywhere with commercial television and enough people with disposable income.

I was determined to go as fast as possible around the rest of Europe, and then the rest of the world.

That became my dream and my goal. My whole business model was about to change.

7

A ROLLER-COASTER RIDE

*Success consists of going from failure
to failure without loss of enthusiasm.*

—Winston Churchill

I was going to expand our operations throughout Europe, and I had set myself the target of doing it in only ninety days. Once I've set my mind to something, it becomes my entire focus. Goals are to be attained, not shunted aside just because they're difficult.

In short order, I found out we could add multiple audio tracks to the same video signal. We quickly created eight different audios, and each local cable operator would simply select the appropriate language for its audience.

We changed the call-in-to-order phone number at the end of the show to a list of sixteen different national flags—England, France, Italy, Sweden, the Netherlands, and so on, with a different phone number alongside each. We paid our British call center to hire people who could take the calls in each of the different languages.

Sales went through the roof. We were doing four times the orders we had projected, which created another problem: fulfillment. In London, we contracted out all fulfillment. Shipping across national borders was expensive, complicated, and time-consuming, requiring customs clearance for each country. We had to find a better way to handle the international orders, and we had to do it fast.

The success we were enjoying in Europe meant that everybody, even Guthy-Renker, began licensing their shows to us because no one else had an operation like this. In no time flat, we were running a hundred products. My Philadelphia banker said to me, "This is sophisticated; it's huge. You've got to have good advice. You need to hire the right representation and the right legal counsel." I signed up with the global management consulting firm of Coopers & Lybrand.

Throughout these pages, I share my views about the value of industry organizations. The Direct Marketing Association had a timely convention coming up in Switzerland, across the lake from Geneva. I went, gathered information on fulfillment and phone centers throughout Europe, and sent Coopers & Lybrand stacks of brochures. I told them to set up a conference call, with me on one end and someone from their office in each European country on the other.

On the call, I asked questions like, "How quickly can we get set up in Germany?"

The answer to that one was, "From six months best case to perhaps a year."

"Why?"

A representative of this company, who I was paying a huge fee to, explained that I would need to establish a separate business in each of sixteen countries. The Germany expert explained that they would have to complete all the required forms for obtaining government approval to open a new business. And, in addition, I would have to post $75,000 for a business license or have that much money on deposit in a German bank.

Others chimed in that I would need more or less the same in each country.

As the bottom-line cost for their services, plus the fees to the various governments, I should be prepared to spend around a million dollars, minimum.

I said, "I want to find a way to be up and running in ninety days, and I can't afford to spend anything like a million dollars."

"Impossible," they said. Their attitude seemed to be, "This Yankee kid is wet behind the ears."

After the call, my team was very discouraged. We had all been walking around with bright stars in our eyes over the idea that we would beat the entire direct-response industry to the punch by establishing an international operation before the rest of the pack had even begun to think about the possibilities.

An entrepreneur has to think outside the box. I began pushing myself for a solution—and was struck by another eureka moment: I was planning to sign up fulfillment companies in each country, outfits already established in business. Why not let each act as the seller of the goods in their own country, with me selling them the products as a wholesaler? That way I wouldn't need all those business licenses.

I called Coopers & Lybrand and described the scheme. "Operating that way, how soon could I be in business?"

The answer came back, "You could be in business tomorrow."

Now we were talking. I asked them to set up contacts for me so that we could buy time from each country's stations. That would still leave me the challenge of selecting the fulfillment centers and phone centers in each country and establishing a relationship with a bank in each.

One of the first meetings I had was in Almelo, outside of Amsterdam, door-to-door something like a seven-hour trip by plane and car from London. I visited there to see one possible fulfillment center and, the next day, was on my way to Munich, only a little over an hour by air but three times that when you include the trips to and from airports plus the airport waiting time. These places were big, sprawling facilities out in the countryside. One man I was visiting mentioned that it was a shame I couldn't fly in, because there was an airport just six minutes from his facility. A lightbulb went off.

Having given myself only three months to get set up, I had to be able to move more quickly than driving from one country to another. The answer: charter a six-seater aircraft. That created a problem: flying was miserable for me. I get airsick.

I stocked up on airsick pills but was still left trying not very successfully to hold down my food. Despite all that, I was still hitting two or three countries a day, landing close to each fulfillment center on my list. I was looking for people who could handle the whole ball of wax—phone calls and fulfillment. In some countries, there simply didn't seem to be any outfit to handle all of it, which meant many more negotiations and contracts to deal with. I was airsick and under tremendous pressure, but I was also enjoying the high of success. I still needed to spend time running the U.S. operation out of Philadelphia, visiting various U.S. cities to find new products and for product development meetings, and traveling to Europe about ten days a month. It meant being away from home at least three weeks a month and working sixteen-hour days even when I was home. My son was still a baby, so it wasn't as if he was missing me on his birthdays or Little League games; still, the pressure on my family life was tough.

My wife wasn't supportive of all the traveling or the long hours. There were a lot of arguments about it, and I tried to explain that I didn't intend to work this hard for my entire life, but right now, I had to seize the moment. That explanation didn't melt the ice with her.

The definition of any entrepreneur is that you work longer than 9 to 5. It's important to have a spouse who understands that and accepts it, working with you as a partner for mutual success. I didn't have that.

Despite all the headaches, the hard work paid off. By the end of my ninety-day time frame, we were completely set up in fifteen countries—call centers, fulfillment centers, banks, the whole nine yards. And 80 percent of the centers worked out; only 20 percent had to be replaced.

What we learned became our framework for future growth. And talk about growth: we thought we'd do about half the volume of what we did in the United States. If the first hour after an airing brought a hundred calls in the States, we estimated we'd do fifty overseas. Instead, the calls were coming in at a rate of three hundred an hour.

From 1990 to 1995, the company revenues soared from $100 million to $400 million.

However, there was a "but" that I hadn't yet recognized again:

In business, growing fast is a pleasure; growing too fast can be a curse.

BEEFING UP THE MANAGEMENT

One day in early 1990, my accountant came in to see me. He said, "Do you ever look at your returns?"

It seemed an odd question. We had set up a continuity selling program, like the Book of the Month Club: when customers joined, they'd get a free Ginsu set, and then each month would receive a new product from us, with the right to return it any time in the next thirty days and receive their money back.

But I had my hands full, as usual, with finding new products, getting the shows produced, and all the rest—plus now, on top of that, running the fledgling operation in Europe. And the bigger and more successful we got, the greater the worries over cash flow: the money, as ever, was going out to pay for media time and product as fast as it came in. ⌐

So why did he think I would be paying any attention to returns?

"One woman," he told me, "has received $10,000 of credits from you for returns. Another has received $26,000." An investigation soon revealed that these two and several others were relatives of our trusted receptionist. How could this be! The warm, friendly lady in the front lobby who had such a welcoming smile was a crook?! She was accepting my bonuses and gifts at the holidays at the same time she was picking my pocket?

I felt violated. I couldn't even bring myself to confront her. And an investigation turned up two accomplices in the accounting department. Looking back, I suppose I should have called the cops and pressed charges. I couldn't quite cope with the idea of sending that lady to prison. Call me a fool or a softy, but I fired them, and we all got back to work. Meanwhile my head of accounting said, "You need to get somebody smarter than you about operations and finance." Obviously.

My search for the right somebody soon led me to a pillar of the local community, a country-club type named Pete Albert. He came with impeccable credentials as the founder and former president of Tampa's Meridian Mortgage Bank, which he had developed into a highly successful purchaser and reseller of real estate mortgages. I had my CPA firm vet his credentials and interview him; they gave a strong thumb's-up.

Jovial, balding, good-looking, and usually with a smile, Pete was a fifty-something socialite who came to work in golf slacks and a golf shirt and seemed like an apt fit for Quantum Marketing, a man who could put us onto a more sound, more businesslike footing. He pointed out that we had no benefits package, no computer staff, no human resource function, no office manager, and very little reporting—all too true. Once he understood what we were doing and how quickly we had grown, he told me, "This is the most amazing thing I've ever seen. This is history. I want to be part of it."

His goal, Pete said, would be to create an organizational structure. He suggested coming on board for a ninety-day trial period, "to see if you like me and to see if I like you." I agreed to give him a salary of $180,000, and if we both agreed, he would stay on after the trial period, and the deal would be sweetened with a 10 percent stake in the company. He would have the title of president and would take over the duties of running the company. I would remain CEO and chairman of the board. I told him that my brother Tim and I were staying with the company, but that he could change anything else that needed to be changed.

As Pete described the situation to one of Professor Churchill's researchers, he found we weren't well organized. "My goal was to take the company from an inspirational seat-of-the-pants growth orientation to a management atmosphere."

It was reassuring to have a solid professional taking over, leaving me to focus on the things I do best.

LAUNCHING A TRADE ASSOCIATION

In 1990 I got a call from a producer for CBS News, who wanted to interview me about the state of the electronic retailing industry. I said there were better people to talk to about the subject, but I'd be willing to be interviewed. Once they were set up and the cameras were rolling, he thrust a microphone in my face and began asking questions about some outfit in the industry that had recently been fined something like $6 million by the FTC, and didn't that mean consumers couldn't trust the claims made in infomercials.

I tried to answer a few of his questions and then gave up. "You said you wanted to talk about the state of the industry," I told him. "I don't have any knowledge about people who have crossed the line in this business any more than what I've read in the papers." There are probably a few bad apples in every industry, but for all I knew, the man who had been fined was an honorable businessman who had broken a rule he didn't even know about.

Electronic retailing was under a cloud in some quarters, in part because of stories like the one the CBS reporter was trying to do, which are good when they make people cautious but can also rob sales from businesses that deal honorably. At the time, I was trying to raise money for the business; after a couple of encouraging meetings with the bank, I was told one of the senior officers began wondering out loud, "Isn't that the industry where people are being charged for merchandise they never got?" The whole industry was being tainted with an unsavory reputation.

Forbes magazine wanted to interview me. That's a highly reputable journal, one I admired. I spent three hours with the reporter they sent and found her very professional. I sat for a session with their photographer. When the issue showed up in the mail, the headline on the story read something like, "Is This a Scam Industry?" The only good news was that the reporter understood I was honest and honorable, and so kindly hadn't used my name.

Not long after, I ran into Greg Renker. We traded stories about how the press was tainting our industry. One of us—I don't even remember which one—said, "If we don't form a self-policing organization, the government may start regulating us." After some checking around, we found a Washington, D.C., law firm, Venable, Howard and Civiletti, that had a big reputation for helping trade organizations get off the ground. They would be happy to take us on—but it wasn't going to be inexpensive.

Greg and I started calling around to friends in the business we thought might be in a position to support the effort. We found several willing to kick in start-up money. Greg and I anteed up $40,000 each and told the law firm to get started. We selected an administrator and a secretary for the new trade group that would eventually come to be called the Electronic Retailing Association (ERA)—still today the principal watchdog outfit for the industry.

Meanwhile Venable, Howard and Civiletti set up meetings for Greg and me with a number of congresspersons to make them aware of the new organization. They also set up a meeting with the Federal Trade Commission, and we found those folks very happy that an industry they were growing concerned about would have an association setting up ethical standards, requirements for lab studies to support the claims made in infomercials, and the rest.

Through the years ERA has grown in strength and effectiveness to become arguably the most influential and respected organization of its kind, now with seven thousand members in forty-three countries. As founders, Greg and I were granted membership for life on the board of the association.

SOARING!

The Beverly Hills operation was going gangbusters. Earl Greenberg was on track to make QMI into a high-quality producer of infomercials, the most polished, professional-looking shows in the industry. Of course, quality comes at a cost. We had been turning out half-hour productions for $25,000 to $75,000 apiece. Earl told me, "I'm going to build the most kick-ass kitchen set you ever saw." And did he ever, with appliances like the top-of-the-line Sub-Zero refrigerator. He hired Screen Actors Guild talent as well as directors and cameramen who had worked on important motion pictures.

In Europe, our operation was doing unbelievable business. The problem was keeping our fulfillment contractors supplied with enough product. We were selling four items, moving tens of thousands of units a week, which we now had to keep stocked in sixteen different warehouses. As always in this business, we had to pay our suppliers in advance, and they had to get the stuff onto ships or airplanes for delivery across the Atlantic. We were on the way to becoming a $500 million company, but even so, having enough money on hand to pay up front for products was a never-ending challenge.

At least the company was becoming more professional, thanks to the efforts of our new president. Pete found that our liability insurance wasn't anywhere near enough to protect us if some product turned out to have a defect—like Apple's problem with one model of the Macintosh computer that for a number of customers inconveniently burst into flames. Pete shored up our management reports and gave Coopers & Lybrand the additional assignment of reviewing our records and setting up a cash-flow and order system.

In those days, and still today, I meet with everyone who describes a product idea that sounds halfway reasonable. I've set a policy that no one else on staff can turn away a product, because I've found that my judgment about this is more reliable. I always want to meet the early-stage inventors, and see for myself what these fledglings have to offer. And if I decide it's not a strong enough product for us, I always give a soft letdown and invite the person to get in touch again if he or she has another possible product for us to consider. And I try to offer advice: "This doesn't work for us, but if I were you, this is what I would do." I've had people come back to me as much as twenty-five years later with another product of their own or something they've run across that they think I might be interested in.

A guiding principle of mine has always been to keep the company lean by hiring outside call centers, fulfillment centers, credit card processing firms, and so on. Pete discovered we were sending huge amounts of money down the drain by operating this way. He started building up in-house units to take over these operations, and he brought in programmers to build software for giving us fast reports on everything that was happening.

THE HOME SHOPPING NETWORK

Some companies can be demanding to work with, and the Home Shopping Network is one of them. Maybe it's because the HSN people labor under so much pressure, or maybe it's the culture of the whole company. Someone with a product to present might fly for eight hours on three different airplanes to get there, only to be told, "I can only give you fifteen minutes."

My experience with HSN has happily been different. I had gone in one day in 1987, met with a couple of their buyers, and was lucky enough to run into the president of their Celebrity Division, Ben White. He and I hit it off big time, and through him I met HSN chairman Roy Spear.

Roy had started as a prosecutor and then had become the owner of a radio station. When a local appliance store went bust owing Roy money for radio ads, the man asked if he would settle for merchandise. Roy looked around and said something like, "I'll take those two cases of can openers. I'll put them on the radio and see if I can blow them out."

A station announcer named Bob Circosta went on the air as "Bargain Bob" with the pitch that "We've got some of these beautiful can openers that usually sell for $29.95, but the first twenty-four people who get down to the radio station can have one for $2.95." Roy was on the phone in short order asking the appliance store owner, "Can you get me another five cases of can openers?"

From that beginning, Home Shopping Network was born. By the late seventies, HSN was a national cable channel in its own right, and by the eighties they were airing internationally.

When I started doing business with HSN, I kept running into Roy. He'd always say something like, "One of these days I'm gonna buy your company."

Since starting Quantum, I had become used to living always on the brink as far as cash flow was concerned. Now, with the added expenses of Europe and Beverly Hills, the money crunch was more intense than ever. The company needed an injection of operating capital.

Or it needed to be in the hands of another outfit flush with cash. That eager old brute Roy Spear was naturally at the top of my list. When I called him to suggest the possibility he said, "Well, let's sit down and talk about it."

I went in to see him, we negotiated for a while, and in the end cut a deal for him to buy Quantum for $10 million. He wanted me to continue running the company, which was fine with me—I would now continue having all the fun with the added plus that I would be free of financial pressures. And on top of that, of course, even after cutting up the pie to give Tim and Pete their slices, I'd still come out a multimillionaire. Home Shopping Network put out a press release announcing the acquisition, while their lawyers and my lawyers began the process of working out all of the nitty-gritty.

Life was good.

Roy wanted to meet the rest of the management team, so I had Earl Greenberg fly in from the coast, and the following week I went back to HSN with Earl and Pete Albert and a couple of the other key people.

Earl came on strong, dropping a whole stream of celebrity names into the conversation. He knew the Vanna Whites and the Cindy Crawfords, and he was going to bring every celebrity into HSN who had ever walked the earth. Roy was soaking it all in, loving it, really impressed with Earl and my whole team.

At the end of the day, when it was time to leave—this was on a Friday afternoon—Earl said, "You don't mind if I stay the weekend? This is going to be great. I might even think about moving from LA to here, so I'd like to stay and check out the area."

The request wasn't as innocent as it sounded. Months later I would find out that Earl and Roy spent a lot of time together over that weekend. My one-year initial contract with Earl would be coming to an end in a few months. Maybe this kind of thing is common in Hollywood, but it wasn't even in my realm of imagination: Earl talked Roy into putting the Quantum purchase on ice. In the end, the acquisition never happened.

Quantum didn't get the infusion of cash, and I didn't have a few million dollars to put into the bank.

COMING INTO THE LIGHT

The picture wasn't very pretty back home in Philadelphia, either. When the end of Pete's first ninety-day trial period was coming up, we both wanted to continue the relationship. Under our agreement, he was now to receive 10 percent ownership in the company. He asked for 20 percent.

I like people who stand behind their contracts. On the other hand, there was no doubt that he had taken over a great deal of the day-to-day decision making and was getting the company running smoothly, allowing me to focus on the creative areas and deal making, where I'm best and happiest. I agreed to give him the additional 10 percent.

This next part isn't easy to admit. I hadn't paid any attention to all the construction going on down the hall from our offices, so you can imagine it came as a great shock one day when I was showing visitors around to discover that my own company had rented the entire remainder of the floor. Offices were being put in for the just-hired in-house lawyer (we were paying him $100,000, a huge savings from the $500,000 we had been paying the firm we hired him from), the new CFO, the new IT staff, the new human resources person (who was already asking to hire a second HR professional to work under her), our own media department, and the in-house software developers, whose made-to-order financial control program never did work.

When I confronted Pete, he said, "Last year we made $85 million. At the current run rate, we're making $100 million this year. Next year we'll make $150 million. We need to build the infrastructure to handle it." When you hire an expert, you should be ready to listen to his advice—right? But where would this take us?

BREAKDOWN

I found a house in the Huntington Valley–Meadowbrook part of Philadelphia, on two acres of land. Essentially brand-new, it had been built for a man who now needed to sell in a hurry. The asking price was $1.3 million; he was willing to part with it for $765,000 if I would guarantee to close in thirty days, with no contingencies. I talked to the bank and got the mortgage paperwork started, signed the contract, and handed over a personal check for $365,000 as a deposit.

At the last minute, the bank wanted some additional inspection or paperwork—I don't recall what this was about, maybe termites or a final visit by a city building inspector or something, which they said would take an additional week. My real estate broker said, "You're in default if you don't close on time," meaning that I would lose the entire $365,000 I had put down.

It would only be a matter of days before the bank would release the funds for my mortgage; meanwhile, I needed

$400,000 to avoid defaulting. I didn't seem to have many options, but since Quantum was a Subchapter S corporation, the money in the bank account belonged to me. My wife Amy and I went to the closing, I handed over a Quantum check for the additional $400,000, we signed the papers, and we received a full deed to the house.

A week or ten days later, my banker phoned to say they were ready to move ahead and the funds were on tap to be transferred as soon as the papers were signed. I would now be able to return the $400,000 to the Quantum bank account, ending the financial pressures the company had been under since I took that money out for the house purchase. The thought that we would once again have working capital was almost enough to make me laugh out loud like a giddy schoolboy. I told Amy when and where we needed to show up for the signing.

Amy said, "We paid cash for the house. We don't need a mortgage."

I said, "Of course we do. That four hundred grand was my working capital from the company."

Her answer was, "F— you. I'm not signing any mortgage."

I figured she was just trying to get under my skin, let me worry, and stew for a few hours. The entire company was at stake. If I lost the company, she would suffer as well. Of course she would show up for the signing.

She didn't.

 Instead of preparing to open a bottle of good champagne, I was suddenly in a deep pucker situation. But I'm a glass-is-half-full kind of guy. For any challenge in business and in life, there is often a solution, once you get over the emotions and start looking for options.

Pete Albert to the rescue—he told me he'd go to the bank and ask for a line of credit.

As a man who knew everybody there was to know in the local banking community, Pete didn't have to work very hard to convince our bank that they should set up a $3.2 million credit line to fund our product purchases and media buys. It took him no time to make those arrangements. All the bank wanted was a $400,000 lien on the house to protect their interest, with the rest of the amount unsecured, just on the basis of the business they knew we were doing, with all the cash passing through their hands.

Whatever Amy's objection had been to signing a mortgage was now behind us. This new document wasn't a mortgage; it was simply a lien on the house that would have no significance for a company rolling in money.

I should have known she wasn't going to see it that way. I tried to explain that the hundred-million-dollar-a-year Quantum could implode without this money. She didn't care. I pleaded, cajoled, shouted, threatened. She said she wouldn't sign. I said I would divorce her. She was unmoved.

We woke up that morning, and I said, "I'll see you at noon at the closing."

She answered, "My lawyer told me not to show up."

I didn't even know she had a lawyer.

At 10:30 that morning, an hour and a half before we were supposed to be at the signing, her lawyer called to say that my wife would show up and sign the papers for an extra 10 percent of the company. As my wife, under Pennsylvania law, she owned an equal share with me. What she was asking for was a controlling interest in the company I had built and was putting in twelve or sixteen hours a day to run.

I went to the closing and sat there until one o'clock. She didn't show. I went home, packed up, and moved out. My attorney filed the divorce papers a week later.

We never did get that $3.2 million line of credit.

In the months following Saddam Hussein's invasion of Kuwait in August 1990 and the U.S. retaliation that came to be known as the Gulf War, world oil shipments from the Middle East plummeted. American motorists sat in long lines to fill their tanks, while gas prices climbed to levels that wouldn't be seen again for almost two decades. Amid gloomy forecasts about the economy, consumers stitched up their pocketbooks.

If Quantum had remained a lean operation, outsourcing for most everything we needed, our costs for the call center operation, credit card processing, legal services, and all the rest would have shrunk at the pace of our declining sales. Instead, we had those hundred people on staff, with benefit programs, health care, and all the other trappings of a large corporation. The situation was desperate.

Sales were down 30 to 40 percent in the United States and Europe. It was like walking across thin ice while the sun is shining. We broke through and slid into the water.

Our fledgling continuity program had been tested for four

months; during that time, just 20 percent of club members returned the merchandise. The finance department did an analysis revealing that even if as many as 30 percent of club members returned the item, we'd still make millions a year. I trusted that analysis. Big mistake. Once we rolled out the full program, returns soared to 55 percent.

Our tough cash-flow situation had become critical.

BAD TO WORSE

After our acquisition by Home Shopping Network had fallen through, I had gone looking for other buyers. Suddenly rescue had become a now-or-never necessity. The most likely prospect I had found was a company called National Media, a competitor of ours in the direct response business, grossing about $85 million a year.

I went in to them proposing that they provide some cash to keep Quantum solvent, in exchange for a minority interest in the company. John Turchi, the chairman, had a counteroffer. "Why don't we just buy you?"

Turchi was a big guy, six-four, gray hair, with a big scar that ran down his chin, said to be from a beer-bottle fight in a bar years earlier. I have no idea whether he really had connections to the mob, as rumors had it, but he had lent money to National Media and ended up being named chairman.

All I knew was that he was treating me fairly, and he offered a fair deal. I would sell Quantum to National Media for

$8 million—some in cash, but mostly in stock. Once again I was poised to be megamillions rich.

To say that National Media's John Turchi and my Pete Albert didn't get along is an understatement. I can work with just about anybody, as long as the person is capable and honorable in their dealings. My golf-club CEO and my bar-fight rescuer couldn't stand each other.

One day, Turchi told me that he had issued a press release announcing that he was pulling out of the deal. As if that wasn't enough, there was one more kicker that happened almost simultaneously. A person on our staff, who was receiving the notices of customer returns forwarded from our processing house, was supposed to issue a credit card refund for each return. But the return notifications were arriving by the mailbag-full, and he was "busy with other things." Without saying anything to me or anyone else, he was throwing all the notifications into a box, meaning to attend to them when he had time. You know where this is leading: customers started complaining to their credit card companies, and the companies began issuing refunds and debiting our bank account by issuing "chargebacks."

The bank started paying attention to these chargebacks just about the time that Turchi announced he was withdrawing his offer to buy Quantum. Was that a coincidence, or had Turchi whispered in someone's ear, in hopes of forcing me into an impossible financial situation, allowing him to swoop in and "rescue" Quantum by taking over the company for $1 or $2 million instead of the $8 million price we had set earlier? If he actually did do that, there would have been nothing illegal about it; it wouldn't even have been entirely unethical. As the old saying puts it, "All's fair in love and war." And business.

Once the bank became aware of all the chargebacks, they understandably grew nervous. Alarm bells started going off. If I had been president of the bank, I'd probably have been hearing alarm bells, too. "We don't deal with chargebacks this high," they said.

I came in one Monday morning, and Pete met me in a panic. "We have a problem." The bank called and said they'd taken $2 million out of our account as additional reserves; instead of a $2 million balance, they were showing us with zero balance. What's more, they would be grabbing every dollar that came into the account and holding all the new money as additional reserve.

That threw everything into turmoil. The bank was refusing the checks we had sent out to stations and product manufacturers and everyone else. Our checks were now bouncing all over the place. It's amazing how quickly word spreads. All the suppliers of our merchandise and all the television stations started refusing our orders unless paid in advance. The word on the street was that we were done.

We were out of money, and the whole company went into a tailspin.

Our lawyers sent a demand letter to the bank arguing that the $2 million hold was a violation of the terms of our agreement with them, but the bank stood firm. I tried to explain that I couldn't see any way out other than filing Chapter 11 bankruptcy, which would force them to release the hold. My banker said I was bluffing, that we were "the hottest game in town," and there was no way I'd file. And even if I did, he said, the terms of the agreement I had signed with the bank meant the court could not order them to release the hold.

⌈Up until a few days before, we had been grossing $100 million a year—$2 million a week. Suddenly we were completely strapped, totally and entirely out of options.⌋

In despair, I told our lawyers to go into court and file Chapter 11. Unlike a Chapter 7 bankruptcy, Chapter 11 allows a company to continue operating, at the same time freezing all creditor claims and demands for payment while a judge monitors the situation and decides who gets what.

Everybody loves to see the big guy go down. People don't care about the explanation of what went wrong; they just love to see the fall. I felt humiliated, all the more because I had just recently been announced as the runner-up for national recognition as the Ernst & Young "Entrepreneur of the Year."

Not only that, but the case study being prepared for the MIT/*Inc.* magazine/Young Entrepreneurs program was now going to be based on a company that had just filed Chapter 11. The brilliant young businessmen flying into Boston for the Birthing of Giants course were going to turn me into a laughingstock. I called Verne to break the news. But I told him I was aiming to pull the company out in time for the MIT program—though at the time I had no idea how that might happen.

Much later he told me that his reaction was, "Well, this is Kevin. He's been through massive ups and massive downs; let's not bet against him." When he told Professor Churchill about my call, Verne added, "When Kevin says something, you believe it. It's the force of his personality." For the two of them, the next few weeks were nail-biters.

Once the Chapter 11 papers were filed with the court, the noose around my neck loosened a tiny bit. All transactions of the past ninety days were unwound—a provision of Chapter 11 that's intended to prevent a business from siphoning cash before filing. For us, this brought the benefit that creditors were ordered by the court to return payments we had made to them in that ninety-day period.

The trauma was tough, but I told myself that life goes on. Ted Turner had hit bottom; Donald Trump has faced severe financial difficulties. It happens. Some days you get the bear; some days the bear gets you. *We are profitable*, I kept telling myself; we were doing $100 million a year.

One of the hardest things to face was that my company president was a banker. How had he let this happen? In hindsight, I should have made Pete Albert chief operating officer instead of president and CEO. That way, he would have had to come to me for major decisions. One of my problems has been that I always give way too much rope. In this case, my CEO, never having run anything but a mortgage bank before, lacked some of the business smarts that turned out to be essential.

It's important to have the right people in place, but you have to stay hands-on. Give rope, but stay on top of the decisions being made.

There's another lesson as well:

> Be careful about putting too much trust in someone who's only been in business during an up cycle. He or she may not know what precautions to put into place so that the business can continue to function when an inevitable down cycle hits.

I told myself that if I used the energy, knowledge, and perseverance to get out of this that I had used to build the business, I'd be fine. I held my head high every day. We weren't out of business; we were a profitable company. We just needed capital. Verne was on the phone often, nervous that I wouldn't be able to save the company and pull out of the mess we were in. I kept telling him, "I'm close. I'm close."

Despite our having turned out a string of wildly successful shows, Quantum was on the chopping block.

And each day in Chapter 11, the company was worth less. I went into court and made a persuasive case that Quantum needed to be sold. The judge agreed: he would announce that the company was up for auction. I pleaded for an early date and managed to persuade the judge to set the auction for a day crucial to me: a Friday in June, the day before the final session of the Birthing of Giants course at MIT.

AUCTION

Even though National Media's Turchi rubbed my CEO the wrong way, and even though he may have been trying to force me into unloading the company to him at a fire-sale price, I still saw him as the best bet for buying the company; as someone already in the infomercial business, he understood the rather unusual business model better than anyone else. Besides, he recognized my value to the company and would almost certainly want to honor the employment agreement that I had signed, which obligated me to stay with Quantum and obligated Quantum to continue me in my role.

To make sure it was a real auction, I drummed up two other bidders: my old nemesis Ira Smolev of Synchronal, and Arthur Toll, a man who had made megabucks in the 1-900 phone business. On the day of the auction, Smolev dropped out early, leaving Toll and Turchi to go back and forth. The bid hit $3 million and kept going up, but in tiny increments—$3.1 million, $3.2, $3.3. The judge was allowing each side time to consider its next bid, the day was dragging on, and I was in turmoil over the possibility of being under the thumb of Ira again, this time on even worse terms. If he had tried to take advantage of me the last time around, what would life be like if he actually owned my company?

The bankruptcy judge was used to auctions of companies that weren't worth a great deal more than the value of the merchandise in their warehouse or storeroom and whatever their desks and computers and so on would bring. This seesaw bidding for a company that had limited assets bewildered him. At one point he asked, "What is it that makes this company so valuable?" I knew. On the prospects just of the products we were already running infomercials on, the company was worth vastly more than these guys were offering. And the auction had turned into a war of two big egos.

The back-and-forth bidding competition lasted the entire day. Finally Turchi won for National Media, at $4.6 million in cash and assumption of $1.5 million in debt. The $4.6 million went to the court to distribute to creditors.

I got half a million in cash. I was confident Turchi would want me to continue running the company, which turned out to be what happened. He also graciously signed over just shy of 2 million shares and options in National Media. At the time, the stock was trading at about $1.45. With the Quantum business added to the mix, the price eventually reached $20 per share, and my stake put tens of millions of dollars into my pocket. At last.

The Birthing of Giants

The Verne Harnish and Professor Neil Churchill "Birthing of Giants" course started on a Wednesday night. Ted Leonsis, who would become the number-two man at AOL, was in that first class, along with others who would become highly successful in their businesses.

I was supposed to be there Friday night and do a question-and-answer session on Saturday. The court session ended late on Friday; I caught the first flight to Boston the next morning.

Verne was waiting for me when I got to the site. I handed him my copy of that morning's *Philadelphia Inquirer*—with an article on my company coming out of bankruptcy. He was delighted and assured me he would have copies made in time to hand out to every person in the class.

He told me, "Kevin, sit in the back. I'm not going to tell them who you are." Verne is a classic showman. He didn't let on that I was in the room and started out with, "Let's hear your views about what Kevin Harrington has done and the decisions he made."

It was hard to listen to what came next. A lot of people were saying nasty things. "He's an idiot. How could he have done this? How could he have done that?" The class was beating me up left and right, reciting my mistakes that they thought had led to the bankruptcy. And I sat there, burning, aching to defend myself.

Finally, Verne handed out copies of the article and said, "Kevin sold the company for the equivalent of $6.1 million." He gave the class members time to read the article.

Then, very theatrically, Verne stood at the front of the room and said, "Kevin, would you like to tell us the rest of the story?"

Every head turned to look as I stood up. There was a tremendous spontaneous roar, and everyone jumped to their feet, applauding and cheering.

I was overwhelmed by the respect I felt coming at me in waves. I sensed they were all thinking, *That could be me.* It was a very emotional moment. I was on the verge of tears and had a hard time holding them back.

That case study was used at MIT/*Inc.* magazine/YEO Birthing of Giants courses for fifteen years.

PART TWO

HOW YOU CAN BECOME THE NEXT TV MILLIONAIRE

Of course there have been many books about how to succeed in business, plenty of them written by people with far better credentials than I have. But I come at this from a unique perspective, as a guy who has found more products that I've turned into megamillion-dollar sales successes than all but a few other people in the world.

The process I have evolved through the years is based on these steps:

Product development
Due diligence
Creative phase
Production
Operational phase
Market testing
Creative tweaking
Rollout
Back-end marketing

In the next chapters, you'll watch over my shoulder to see how we put these steps into action on a couple of very different products. (Not all steps are included in each discussion—just the ones that were most significant for the particular product.)

8

A FISH STORY

The only people who never tumble
are those who never mount the high wire.

—Oprah Winfrey

Some people don't like the term *networking*, based on the complaint that many of the folks who use networking as a way of trying to get ahead are just out for themselves rather than seeing it as a give-and-take proposition. I have used people at times for my own advantage, and other people have used me for theirs. But my idea of networking is establishing relationships that work both ways. I may call you today for some information or advice or to be put in touch with someone or just to tap your brain and experience. But I'll always be available to do the same kind of favor in return. And even beyond that, if I have respect for who you are or what you're achieving, I'll give you a hand when you ask, even if there's little possibility you would ever be in position to do something for me.

My fish story has a couple of examples of that, beginning with how the whole thing got started. One day a phone call came in from a man I had been keeping in touch with—Jim Caldwell, a narrator and host we had used in a few early shows. He told me he had run into a guy with a product I had to see. What was it? A fishing lure!

I said, "Jim, a fishing lure is a niche product. And what do they sell for? Five dollars?"

"No," he said, "around a buck."

"There's no way I can make money selling a one-dollar item in an infomercial."

"Kevin," he said, "you gotta take this meeting."

I reluctantly agreed, on condition that I might cut the meeting short if it was clear I couldn't do anything for the guy.

He arrived about three days later, a long-haired specimen named Alex Langer, who must have weighed at least 300 pounds. He brought a videotape with him and put it in the player while he explained what was so unique about his lure. He said that if you tell a fisherman about a new type of lure that will catch more fish, he'll buy it—and that there are 80 million fishing licenses issued in the United States every year. Eighty million!

I had no idea if that was correct or just a number he threw out to impress me, but either way I got the point: this is a huge market.

He explained what made his lure so special. When other lures are cast into the water, they drop straight down. "But I have engineered and reverse-rigged a lure that hits the water and *swims away* from where it lands—looking like a wounded fish."

At fishing shows, they demonstrate new hooks and so on by showing them in a long, flat water tank that they call a hog trough. The trough can be thirty feet long and more, and taller than a man, and it's filled with fish. His demo tape showed that an ordinary lure hits the water and sinks to the bottom of the tank, the fish hardly paying any attention. Then the picture switched to show Langer's lure: just as he had said, it hit the water and started swimming away. As if drawn by a magnet, the fish began to turn toward it, watching it swim. One by one, the fish began going after it. I'm no fisherman, but I could hardly believe what I was seeing.

I still couldn't imagine how I would ever be able to market it, yet I was so impressed that I made him an offer: we would develop the product, produce an infomercial, and pay him about a dollar for every kit we sold. He didn't like the deal and said he'd do a television commercial himself.

I guess he was stunned when he found out a half-hour show would cost around $150,000. Instead he did a two-minute commercial, which flopped, and a few months later he was back at my door, pen in hand to accept the deal I had first offered.

It was time for us to launch into our product cycle.

✭ PRODUCT DEVELOPMENT ✭

What do you do with a $1 product to build it out so that people will pay $39.95 for it? I sent a team out to research the industry, going into various kinds of fishing shops and asking the owners, "How would you sell this? How would you position it? What else do fishermen need?" We began to assemble ideas for an entire package, with a group of the new lures, plus sinkers, weights, fishing line, and so on, all neatly packaged in a plastic tackle box that a fisherman could take with him right down to the shore or out in his boat.

✭ DUE DILIGENCE ✭

In our context, due diligence means finding out from experts in the field whether the product really makes sense, whether potential customers will really want it. Who would you ask about a product like this?

If you said, "other fishing lure manufacturers," that's not a very likely source. It's almost certainly a waste of time, because nobody wants to give marketing advice to a competitor.

Any fisherman in your family could tell you that there are a good number of fishing shows on television. The hosts of those shows would be a fantastic source of information and opinion. But how do you get in contact with them?

If you want to reach a television personality, here's how you might go about it: You call the network or station and ask, "Who takes the phone calls for Mr. So-and-so?" If you sound like a professional and not a kook or a fan looking for an autograph, they'll give you the phone number for his agent or manager. You call that person; if the secretary or assistant won't put you through, leave a message with him or her, something like, "Please tell your boss I have something that will make him a huge amount of money. Here's my name and phone number." I've used that method many times. I won't claim it always works, but you'll be surprised how successful you can be with it.

Here's another approach: I once wanted to get together with Gene McCaffery, the chairman of ShopNBC. I checked with a contact of mine in New York, who told me, "Every Wednesday he eats dinner at Elaine's." I sent one of my top people the next Wednesday and managed to persuade a reluctant maître d' to relay his message that a man at another table had asked for five minutes to speak about something that could make money for his network. I don't think McCaffery liked the request, but he agreed, and listened long enough to set up an appointment for me with one of his executives.

On another occasion I had a project that I realized could be big if I could get the participation of someone with an instantly recognizable name. The person at the top of the list I jotted was certainly recognizable: Donald Trump.

Of course, with someone like "the Donald," you don't just dial his company and ask to speak to his secretary. Even if you did manage to get through, unless you also have a famous name, the chance that she would even take a message from you stands at pretty close to absolute zero.

Trump's first book, *Trump: The Art of the Deal,* had just recently been published. It's far easier to track down most authors than celebrities. I had little trouble getting the phone number of the man who had written Trump's book and reaching him on the phone. I said, "I'm in the business of selling on television. I could sell a ton of your books."

He heard me out and said, "I'll get back to you." And he did, the very next day. What he said was, very simply, "Donald wants to see you at two o'clock tomorrow at the Trump Tower." With a single phone call, I had gotten an invitation into the inner sanctum to meet the man himself. I started making travel plans.

Thinking about that meeting still makes me laugh. I walked in frankly a little nervous because I still looked way younger than my real age, which sometimes made it tough for me to be taken seriously, even by people who were a lot more friendly and open-minded than Donald Trump's reputation made him out to be.

Walking off the elevator, I discovered I was standing in Trump's reception area in front of the secretary's desk. She said he was expecting me but was on the phone and would be with me shortly. The door to his office was standing open. I sat down and could hear every word he was saying, and every word he was screaming, which happened more than once. "I told you it was gold, not silver!" and this and that, something or other about one of his buildings. The words coming out of his mouth and the occasional shouting were scaring the hell out of me.

He went on like that for *twenty minutes*. I was thinking, *I could be here all day*. He finally finished that call and took another and then another and then another. And all along what I was hearing showed him to be a tough negotiator, an exacting partner, and a demanding boss—beyond what you've ever heard about Donald Trump.

Finally he *slammed* the phone down on the last call. He appeared in the doorway of his office, looked at me, and said, "Okay, come on in here." By the time I got into his office, he was standing behind his desk. I started to sit down. Pointing a finger at me, he blared, "Don't you dare sit down. Listen, I'm a busy man. I could take another call that would make me a lot of money or solve a problem for me. Before you sit your ass in that chair, I wanna know how much time this is gonna take and how much is my cut going to be—how much do I stand to make?"

It felt like I had just been smacked in the face. How do you respond to something like that?

I managed to keep my wits about me enough to reply, "I need four hours of your time, and you can make $4 million cash, net."

He loosened up and said, "Okay, take a seat."

(The figure I'd given him wasn't pumped up to capture his interest; it was a valid computation. The concept was that I do an infomercial with him to sell his book. I could shoot it in four hours. Based on my experience with how many units of a product we could sell with a powerful show, I figured we should be able to move a million copies of the book, which would put $4 million in his pocket.)

Even to Donald Trump, $4 million for four hours of work apparently sounded like a good deal. After he had listened to the details, he spent the rest of an hour jabbering with me, entrepreneur to entrepreneur. He told me stories about the celebrities he knew and the business deals he was involved in, and I told him about some of my runaway successes with infomercials and which magazine covers I had been on lately. Somewhere during the conversation, I commented, "Donald, you and I should be doing a TV show together." Years later, reality producer Mark Burnett approached Trump about a show that was to become *The Apprentice*, featuring Donald Trump.

In the end, my project with Trump didn't fly. He envisioned people seeing his image on the air at three o'clock in the morning hawking his book. That just wasn't the way he wanted people to be thinking about him.

Still, the story is a good illustration of my point:

You can get yourself in front of important people, people who everyone else would say are totally inaccessible, by letting them know you can make them a lot of money.

✧ CREATIVE PHASE ✧

The creative challenges in a product development and launch can be the most enjoyable and fascinating part of the whole process. But the creativity is an aspect for which most people in business do well to rely heavily on an in-house or outside creative team. We faced several interesting creative challenges on the lure show. For one thing, a check of our overnights revealed just what I expected: no one had ever aired a fishing lure product show on TV in which you could actually see the fish responding. So filming a hog trough to let the viewer see the action of an ordinary lure compared to Alex Langer's lure was a no-brainer. The audience would get to witness what I had seen, how the fish turned to follow the lure and then go after it.

Especially for a consumer product, the question of what to call it is always a critical issue. The name we eventually settled on was the "Flying Lure"—because that's what it looks as if it's doing: flying through the water.

From the wildly enthusiastic responses we were getting when the fishing show hosts and owners of fishing stores had a chance to try the lure for themselves, the basic shape of the infomercial became obvious. This was going to be a half-hour production devoted almost entirely to testimonials.

The following is perhaps too obvious to mention, but I will anyway:

⌐There's no point in designing advertising and promotion in which you praise the product yourself if you can get the believability of enthusiastic real people praising the product for you.⌐

The completed show was to have something like fifty testimonials, including from some of the best-known names in the fishing world, plus ordinary fishing addicts—not just men but also women and youngsters who had tried the lure and had great things to say about their results. The effect was mind-blowing, setting the infomercial apart from anything anyone had done before.

⚜ PRODUCTION ⚜

How do we shoot this show in the studio? Ooops, we can't.

We were a gadget company. The core of all our shows up until then had been shot in the studio, each one scheduled to be done in a single day from the first "Roll camera" to the final "That's a wrap!" This one obviously wasn't going to be believable unless we scheduled it as a location shoot. That meant a budget closer to what Earl Greenberg had been spending, several times any infomercial I had yet done.

This would be my first infomercial since Quantum was taken over by National Media, but the National Media pockets were deep enough that they showed no concern when I told them it would be a fifteen-day shoot on lakes and then the ocean, with a $150,000 production budget.

You've got to commit to doing it right.

✷ MARKET TESTING ✷

If you're manufacturing screwdrivers or shipping crates or kitchen appliances or children's teddy bears, you may find no value in regional testing; those products probably sell as well in Paducah and Oshkosh as they do in New York, Atlanta, La Jolla, and Nashville.

Even so, we always look at test results with an eye for discovering the unexpected. With the Flying Lure, though, I didn't have any reason to think there would be a difference from one part of the country to another. Boy, was I wrong.

To begin with, the product initially looked like a flop. The shows were bringing in sales, but nothing like the volume for a product that's going to turn into a big winner for us. I began to wonder whether I had misjudged the sales potential or whether we might have made some big error in judgment about the packaging, the design of the infomercial, or some other essential factor.

We typically test a new show in New York, LA, Dallas, Miami, Tampa, Atlanta, and St. Louis. On this one, sales were very spotty—strong in some markets, really lousy in others. In some places the sales were five times higher than elsewhere.

What we began to figure out was that a number of our test-market outlets are coastal cities. Lures, we were discovering, are bought more heavily by people who live in lake areas. We quickly began shifting the media buys to places like St. Louis and Cincinnati, Michigan and Missouri—signing up stations state by state and city by city, in places where the lake fishers live, the places where fishing licenses regularly sell in very large numbers.

We also discovered that the best airtimes for the show were on the weekends in the early morning; by afternoon, our potential buyers were already out fishing.

After that experience, I began to wonder how many viable products were dropped by their manufacturers because no one had thought to analyze the market reports.

✰ OPERATIONAL PHASE ✰

Every product we've sold has had some glitch, and this unhappy fact has convinced me it's nearly impossible to get everything right the first time out of the barn. On this one, when the first orders began coming in, and we started shipping the tackle boxes, the customer service lines began to ring—twenty calls one day, thirty calls the next, and pretty soon the phones really began lighting up.

People were complaining that their tackle boxes arrived with holes in them, or that they developed holes after a short period. We checked, and the boxes leaving the warehouse were in perfect condition. What in the world could be going on?

It turned out that the company manufacturing the hooks was protecting them with a coating of oil. The oil, strangely enough, was eating through the plastic of the boxes: the two materials were antagonistic to each other. When my people checked with the manufacturer of the boxes, he said something like, "Oh, you didn't tell me about the oil. I just have to make your boxes out of a higher-quality material." My purchasing people had not thought to ask if the boxes came in different levels of quality, and I guess the manufacturer was used to competitive bids and quoting the lowest price he could, and so he didn't even think to mention that there was a choice to consider.

The problem was easily fixed, but the cost of refunds and replacement of boxes eventually ran into the hundreds of thousands of dollars.

Before you ship a million units of that new product, keep asking your head of customer service or your outsourced customer service manager about the calls they are getting. That's your early warning system for changes that need to be made in the product's design or packaging.

✛ CREATIVE TWEAKING AND ROLLOUT ✛

As we often do, we started by running the show in different cities, offering the product at different price points. Even though the package we had put together had twenty of the Flying Lures and a total of something like fifty other items, we quickly found that $39.95, the price point justified by the contents, wasn't viable. The sales at $29.95 were so much stronger that it settled the price question: $29.95 it would have to be. When you find the sweet spot, you run with it, even if it means a lower margin.

Once we had settled on the right cities and times for the show, and the right price, the Flying Lure infomercial worked unbelievably well, making it the favorite lure of fishermen (and fisherwomen) worldwide, selling over 200 million units. The inventor, Alex Langer, and the on-camera host for the show, Jim Caldwell, made millions of dollars each, enough to be on easy street for the rest of their lives.

A compelling product, at the right price, promoted by a strong infomercial is a nearly unbeatable marketing combination.

9

WAXING WISE

The most difficult thing is the decision to act;
the rest is mere tenacity.

—Amelia Earhart

Sometimes, unexpectedly, you discover a void in the market, recognizing it yourself or being led to it by someone else. The story of a car wax product was one that came to us from a stranger.

PRODUCT DEVELOPMENT

One day in 1991, a man named Kelvin Claney came in to tell me about his idea for developing car waxes in all the different popular car colors. He had barely gotten through a couple of sentences before I was asking myself, *Why hasn't someone done this already?* I thought the concept was brilliant. It just seemed like a natural. And, so important in this business, I could already begin to visualize the infomercial.

It was simply obvious: When you go to buy shoeshine polish for your black shoes, you buy black polish; for your brown shoes, you buy brown. If you have any that are red or white or blue, you buy those colors, too.

But back then, if you went to an auto parts store or supermarket to buy car wax, there weren't any colors. For a black car, you bought neutral wax. For a silver car, you bought neutral wax. For a red car, you bought neutral wax.

After a short period of due diligence to be sure there wasn't a product like this already on the market, and that there were no patents that might stand in the way, we worked out a license agreement with Kelvin that would put money in his pocket for every unit sold, and we took over. From there on, we owned the product, we developed it, and we trademarked it.

Choosing the manufacturer wasn't difficult. We had already worked with Innovative Chemical, and I had built a relationship with the boss, Dick Elliot. We went out for competitive bids just because it's appropriate business practice, even when you're dealing with someone you trust.

From the outset it was clear that creating the product line was going to bring some unusual challenges. The first one was deciding how many different colors to offer, and which shade of each. The color of the wax doesn't need to be an exact match to the color of the car, I learned, but even within a single brand of car, black on one model isn't the same as black on another. And you can just imagine the variations of red.

The manufacturer came up with a list of the top-selling colors. From their research and analysis, they determined that sixteen colors would cover 80 to 90 percent of buyers. This was a go/no-go point: if the percentage had been much smaller, we would not be likely to generate enough sales for the effort to be worthwhile, and I would have reluctantly killed the project.

Also, the sixteen colors were critical in another way as well. By this time in our operations, we had recognized that no matter how many calls and orders an infomercial generated, we were only benefiting from part of the response: lots of people didn't place an order because they were planning to go look for the product at Wal-Mart or the local mall. Direct-response advertising generates orders by telephone and mail, but it also sends a lot of people to jot a note on their shopping list for the next time they're hitting the stores.

Retail became a major contributor to our bottom line and a factor for us to consider with every product rollout. This time it would be a particular challenge, because we weren't going to be asking for room for a single product on the store shelves; we were going to be asking for space for every one of the colors we were offering. Sixteen was already stretching the limit of what retailers would want to let us have; if Innovative had given us a number of colors much higher than that, it could have been another killer for the project.

✮ DUE DILIGENCE ✮

How do you make certain that you can trust what the developer or manufacturer tells you about the effectiveness and safety of the product? If you want to stay in business, you won't just take their word for it.

Almost every one of the hundreds of products we've marketed through the years has gone through a two-stage process of ensuring that buyers won't be harmed and that no large numbers will be dissatisfied. (No matter what the product, it's almost an absolute certainty that *some* buyers will be unhappy. It's simply human nature.)

The first stage is evaluation by a product testing facility. If the item is mechanical—such as, say, the Stair Stepper—is it made with materials heavy enough that it won't break in normal usage? If it's a beauty product, does it burn the skin or cause discoloring or in any other way do harm? If it's a product with emissions like our rodent repelling device, does it meet the applicable FCC requirements? And what happens if a baby sits down in front of the rodent repeller, or chews on it? The testing lab will also, of course, put the product through its paces to measure whether it lives up to the claims about building abs or reducing wrinkles or keeping rodents away.

This testing may take months, in some cases even a year or longer, sometimes involving a back-and-forth between the lab and the manufacturer: "We find a problem with this aspect; can you come up with a work-around?"

Only when that part of the process has been finished will the next part get started, in which a specialized law firm or attorney reviews the lab reports and all the product claims. A lawyer with Federal Trade Commission expertise examines the claims against federal truth-in-advertising requirements. For some products, other lawyers examine whether the product meets Food and Drug Administration requirements, and so on.

✐ CREATIVE PHASE ✐

The biggest creative challenge was easy to state but hard to answer: how do you convince people to spend $30 for a product similar to what they had been spending $3 for?

We came up with a stunning way of showing the benefits of colored car wax. The plan was to bring in a yellow Ferrari and, with the cameras rolling, scrape a wide knife all the way down the middle of the hood, scratching off a wide swath of paint, down to the metal. We would then rub the red car wax over the entire car and especially over the scrape. The wax wouldn't turn the car red, but the exposed metal would soak up the color, giving the car a hot, jazzy stripe down the hood. Not that we were trying to encourage anyone to scrape the paint off their car, yet it would be a very dramatic visual demonstration of how the wax bonds magnetically, giving deeper, richer colors—redder reds, yellower yellows—and also fills in scratches and scars, leaving a bright, shiny, like-new surface, looking even better than if the car had been repainted.

This is a great example of what we call a "money shot." Very few people turn on their television set to watch an infomercial. You're flipping through channels looking for something that captures your interest. When you come to an infomercial, most likely you keep right on going. Only if there's something on screen that's visually arresting will you stop on that channel and watch. So an infomercial needs to have something visually interesting going on as much of the time as possible.

A money shot goes beyond being just visually interesting. It's a few moments in the show when we try for something so catchy that people won't just enjoy it, they'll tell their friends. A great money shot is something so astounding or so gripping that you remember it and talk about it.

In one car wax show we had done with Kelvin, we had set fire to a Rolls-Royce to prove how the wax protected it. The demonstration was powerful enough to sell tons of the wax. In another car wax infomercial, we hired a stunt driver who drove the car through a tunnel of flame. (Another money shot example: For the Flavor-Wave oven from Korea, we cryogenically froze two rib roasts to minus 360 degrees, then dropped one of them from thirty feet and showed how it smashed into a thousand pieces; the other one, frozen just as solid, we put into the Korean oven and showed it coming out an hour later, tender and juicy, cooked all the way through.)

The final creative elements I'll mention here were choosing

the product name and selecting the on-camera host. After considering a list of clever and catchy names, we ended up picking one that was more practical and descriptive: Colorcote Car Wax.

As for the host, the danger in an infomercial is using a person who seems too slick, so smooth talking that you aren't sure you can trust him. Quite a number of the hosts we've chosen have built a reputation on the recognition they gained from the infomercial. That happened here, too. We selected a dapper, clever man named John Parkin, whose trademark was his bow tie. John became famous from this show. He was frequently stopped on the street like a movie or TV star.

✩ PRODUCTION AND OPERATIONAL PHASE ✩

Next we faced what this product line would mean for our warehouse operation. Sixteen different SKUs (for the uninitiated, that's "stock-keeping units," an inventory-control term), with thousands going out and returns coming back, sounded like more than we were set up to handle. In fact, it sounded like a nightmare.

Instead, we negotiated a deal with the manufacturer to dropship for us (that is, ship directly to the customer), which allowed much better management of inventory: if one particular color was selling fast, they could quickly produce more cases of it; if another wasn't keeping pace in sales, they would hold up running additional units of that color. It would make for a much smoother operation.

✭ MARKET TESTING ✭

In the months of snow and sleet and hail, not too many people think about waxing their cars. They want to wait for a season of buds on the trees and drives to the baseball stadium. When I realized that the car wax show was going to be ready to start airing in October, it set me back. Was it worth spending the money for test airings at a time of year when most people weren't interested in thinking about waxing their car?

Everything was nearly geared up to go, so I decided we'd try some limited test airings. That proved to be a good choice: against expectations, the orders started rolling in.

But the testing phase proved valuable in a couple of other ways, as well. We found that it wasn't good enough for people to order "red." That one particular color turned out to come in too many variations. We were getting angry calls from people whose cars looked a different color red after they applied the wax. So we added a scene at the end of the infomercial with color swatches of the different reds, and told viewers to match their car color to the appropriate swatch, then tell the operator when they called in which number red they wanted.

We always get some product returns and complaints that the

product doesn't work as advertised. All the money spent on laboratory testing and legal review of the lab reports can't guarantee every purchaser will be happy. With most products, all the dissatisfied customer wants is to have his or her money back. It's part of the business; we launch every new infomercial knowing that we'll be sending refunds to some percentage of the purchasers.

In this case, the challenge was somewhat different. If a guy buys the product, uses it on his car, and then calls customer support complaining that the wax has somehow or other ruined the appearance of his Camaro, he's not going to be satisfied by being offered a refund. The solution we came up with was going to be costly, but necessary: every purchaser who appeared to have a legitimate gripe was told that we would pay to have his or her car repainted, and we sent a check for $300 to cover the cost of the job at their local Maaco.

⭐ CREATIVE TWEAKING ⭐

Since the car wax was obviously geared to a male audience, we booked it first into the "male" time slots—focusing on 1:30 and 2:00 in the morning and on weekends. Once I saw that the show was working, I figured, what the hell, let's try it with the women and see what happens. We bought slots on the Lifetime channel. To my delight, women turned out to be eager buyers of the product as well. Some were ordering it for their own use, but most, I suspect, were ordering it as a gift for their husbands or as a hint: "The car isn't looking so great anymore, dear— maybe you should try this."

Sometimes you just don't know what your market is until you try.

✦ ROLLOUT ✦

Colorcote Car Wax turned into a huge product for us, a gigantic winner, both on sales directly from the infomercial and from retail sales generated by the infomercial—altogether selling over 4 million units in the time we handled the product.

Envy can be a compliment. One of the giants of the car wax industry, Shelly Adelman, the founder and head of Blue Coral, called and said, "Who *are* you guys!? How did you manage to come into a market that's been around for years and years and take all this retail space away from everybody?"

I could understand his frustration. In only eighteen months after our first car wax show ran, we had grabbed over 30 percent of the car wax market. That is the power of the infomercial.

But Shelly wasn't really angry. In fact, he hired us to do infomercials for his own products.

PART THREE

ADVICE FROM THE TRENCHES

10

THE MOST OVERLOOKED IDEAS FOR FINDING NEW PRODUCTS AND INCREASING SALES

Men succeed when they realize that their failures are the preparation for their victories.

—Ralph Waldo Emerson

Robert Allen, the real estate guru and author of the best-selling books *Nothing Down* and *Creating Wealth* promotes himself with a line that goes something like this: Put me down inside any city, and within twenty-four hours I'll own a piece of valuable real estate. What he means is that he can find a piece of property that he'll be able to turn around in short order and make a good profit on.

Stealing a page from Allen, I offer my own challenge: Give me twenty-four hours anywhere, and I will come up with a home-run product. By "home-run product," I mean one that isn't selling big when I find it but that I can turn into a giant seller that will put a lot of money in my pocket and a lot of money in the pocket of whomever I make a deal with in order to handle the item.

You can do the same—whether you're a small entrepreneur, an inventor or an innovator, a product person in a larger company, or an individual looking to act as an agent or representative. What Allen does is buy a copy of the local newspaper, look up homes for sale, and drive through neighborhoods checking out what's available until he spots something that meets his criteria.

⚡ GETTING STARTED ⚡

To begin, you're going to assemble the largest stack of recent catalogs you can get your hands on. Then you're going to start going through them, one by one. Obviously you're not going to read all the copy. Instead, flip through the pages, taking in the items on each pair of facing pages, then flip, and on to the next pair.

Unless you have a rather remarkable memory, very little of what you're seeing will register at first. Gradually, more and more of the products will start to stick in your mind.

I've said this earlier: what you're looking for is the same product showing up in three or four or more catalogs. Any product that makes it into several catalogs at the same time is likely to be something that's become a big seller. The catalog companies keep close track of what the other catalogs in their field are carrying. When company X notices that catalog Y has featured the same item in their spring, fall, and winter issues, the buyer at company X figures, "That item must be selling well for them; we need to carry it, too." The buyer then goes out to track down the manufacturer and make arrangements to add the item to company X's catalog.

The buyers are doing your work for you. When you spot an item in several catalogs, it's a sure sign that it's a good seller.

IDENTIFYING THE SOURCE

So you've identified a product you think might be a winner for you. Next problem: how do you find the name of the manufacturer? For the most part, the catalog won't list the name. These days you might be able to find out everything you need simply by Googling the name of the product.

If you draw a blank, here's another way that usually works: simply place an order from one of the catalogs for the sweater or dog leash or whatever the item is. When it arrives, reading the fine print on the package will most often reveal the piece of information you're looking for.

✷ MORE WAYS OF FINDING PRODUCTS ✷

Besides catalogs, which I've mentioned several times, where else do I hunt to find products? Again you may recall the answers from earlier in this book. Three major places: newspapers, magazines, and trade shows.

Since I subscribe to about a hundred magazines, I obviously don't read them cover to cover. My approach is what I refer to as "power reading." The process begins with the table of contents. I scan it, go to the articles that catch my eye, and see which ones I want to spend more time with because I think there is something in them that might point me to a product. I circle the listings of those articles in the table of contents. On Monday morning I'll bring in a stack of maybe thirty magazines with perhaps fifty or sixty articles circled. My secretary will locate each of those articles, tear each out of the magazine, and put them all together in a binder. The following weekend I'll have that binder with me. If the weather is good (as it often is in St. Petersburg, where I now live), I'll sit at the pool or on the beach and scan each of the articles I selected.

I also read several newspapers. One of my favorites is the *New York Times* because I consider their business section second to none. The rest of the paper I'll breeze through, but the business section gets my attention on every page. Returning from a trip, I'll go through the business section of every edition I missed while I was on the road.

Trade shows, of course, I consider to be gold mines. If you're serious about making money in the ways I talk about in this book, the trade shows are an essential. You can go through an event like the Housewares Show in Chicago and walk out of there with ten items that you can present to HSN and the other national direct-marketing television channel, QVC. And once you get the hang of dealing with HSN and QVC, from those ten items you may come away with two or three purchase orders.

There are trade shows in nearly any product category you can name, and they are usually easy to track down with a simple Internet search. There are shows dedicated to fishing, fitness, toys, hardware, housewares, golfing . . . and other specialized categories that would surprise you. (On the other hand, if you're looking for products to float past HSN and QVC, obviously they need to be mass-market items.)

Many of these shows are not open to the public, but the requirements for proving you are connected with the industry are usually not very stringent. Often a business card showing that you're in the trade is all that's needed.

Most people who attend trade shows don't walk the show the way I do. It takes time, energy, and stamina, but I try to see *every* booth. I'm less interested in the central-aisle, megabucks booths with all the glitz and glamour, because the products they're showing are not usually the unheralded items, the little-known or unknown goodies that I can make a deal on for an infomercial or a sale to a shopping channel. Those winners are more often in the outlying rooms, the netherland of low-budget companies and lone entrepreneurs.

When you're working a trade show, be sure to give yourself plenty of time at the "New Products Showcase" (or whatever it might be called). That's where you're most likely to find items that you can run with.

There are plenty of other ways, as well, to find products. Sometimes it just takes inquisitiveness or ingenuity. Several years ago I saw an ad for the Tempur-Pedic mattress. I didn't believe it could be as good as they said, but I have trouble sleeping, so I ordered one. It didn't come cheap; I seem to recall that I paid $2,200.

When the mattress was delivered and I began sleeping on it, I found it unbelievable. I really was getting a much better night's sleep. So naturally I began to wonder what made the mattress so special. This wasn't just curiosity, this was *business* curiosity. I took a sharp knife and actually sliced down the side of my $2,200 mattress.

The ad had said the top of the mattress was made of a special material called "visco-elastic memory foam." When I pulled the siding away enough to see the construction, it was evident that the top three inches were indeed a different material. So what, really, was this "memory foam"?

It turned out to be one of those byproducts of the space program, a material made from polyurethane and other chemicals, developed in a search by NASA for ways to reduce the effects of the intense g-force pressure experienced by astronauts during launch. In the end it never worked well enough in that role to be installed in the space capsules, but other uses were found.

The substance has a quality that makes it a good choice as a mattress material: it's firmer at cooler temperatures, but softens when warmed up. When you lie down on a memory foam mattress, as your body heat warms up the material, the foam gradually conforms to the shape of your body, allowing you to feel more comfortable.

Who makes it? Today I could just do an Internet search; back then, a guide to manufacturers and products called the *Thomas Register* gave me the information I was looking for: memory foam was a material available from a company called Carpenter; the firm was doing a billion-dollar business just on that one material.

There are companies in the United States—and elsewhere, I'm sure—that specialize in doing "parallel development." (When people ask if some product or other that I've marketed is a knockoff, my usual answer is, "No, we did some parallel development." That typically gets a laugh.) Whatever you call it, the process involves the sometimes-annoying practice of coming up with a product suggested by what someone else is already marketing, but different enough that you're not infringing on any patents or trademarks. When Crest comes out with something new in its toothpaste, Colgate will, within a few months, introduce a similar product with essentially the same claims of benefits. That's parallel development.

These specialty labs can take almost any material you come up with and develop a version of similar material for you. And that's what I did with the memory foam. Finding a manufacturer, I ordered pads of foam three inches thick, in all the standard bedding sizes—single, twin, double, queen, king, and California king. As a pad, it can be laid atop your existing mattress, giving you the same comfort as if the mattress were made entirely of the memory foam. This type of top-of-the-mattress pad came to be called a "topper."

We called our product the True Sleeper memory foam topper, and set the price at $200—quite a savings over the $2,200 I had paid, yet producing virtually the same effect. So the product appealed even to people who had bought a new mattress quite recently. Our infomercial said, "You don't sleep on the middle and bottom, just on the top. So you don't need to get rid of your mattress to get a better night's sleep."

The infomercial turned out to be quite compelling—so compelling, in fact, that the product has brought us revenues of more than $260 million, making it one of our top-five products ever.

MAKING THE DEAL

But now that you've identified a few hot-selling items and their manufacturers, how are you going to make them pay off for you? I'll begin to answer that question by telling you a story.

One of my early successes was with a man who made quite an impression from the first. You might recognize the name: Tony Little. Back in 1990, I saw him pitching a product live on the Home Shopping Network. He'd pitch for a bit, in that high-energy, in-your-face, shouting, almost screaming style of his. Then they'd roll a couple of testimonials. Tony would come back again for some more pitch, then more testimonials. I thought, *That's exactly the way we're doing our infomercials, and he'd be a perfect pitchman.*

When I got in touch, it turned out Tony had conceived an exercise device called the Ab Isolator that we both thought was right for an infomercial. We made history together with that product: he first sold it on the Home Shopping Network, I licensed the footage from HSN and ran it as an infomercial, making it the first-ever live infomercial.

I've always preferred controlling all aspects of a product and bearing all the costs. That's what we did here, giving Tony 5 percent of the sales price and putting up the millions it takes to roll out a product. His share may not sound like much, but we sold 7 million units at $35 each.

Through the eighteen years since then, Tony has done infomercials in practically every product category, from other fitness products (the Gazelle exercise device alone brought in sales revenues of over $1 billion), to fitness tapes, pillows, massagers, massage chairs, health drinks, even bison burgers.

Tony's in-your-face, abrasive style doesn't sound like a good way to sell a product, but for him it has definitely worked. Everything he pitches turns to gold. The funny thing is that in person, he's very different—calm and friendly, very caring, very loyal. In fact, off camera he's almost shy. I have sometimes wondered if the yelling and screaming is because he has to do that to overcome his shyness.

Whatever the explanation, the fact is that Tony Little is a phenomenon: one of the best salesmen in the history of television. When I took the product to Home Shopping Network, they agreed to carry it but of course wanted Tony to pitch it himself, meaning he would have to appear in front of the cameras live each time the product was offered. His selling ability, and the requirement that he repeatedly do the live pitch, are the reasons why it made sense to me that he should have the best deal I've ever given anyone: a 50/50 split. When you work with a superstar, you bend the rules.

I spoke to him just this morning, and he was elated: he had just heard the weekend sales figures for the Rock N Roll Stepper. Over the single weekend, despite the country's being in the throes of a recession rivalling the 1930s, the product had produced over $2 million in sales.

As I write this in late 2008, in the preceding three years I have had 150 products on television, and I didn't invent any of them. Every one is a product that I took on under a distribution deal giving me exclusive distribution rights because the product owner didn't know how to connect with HSN or QVC. Call it "putting people together." When you have the contacts or the fortitude and time that other people aren't able to muster, you can grow rich by becoming an agent or representative. You get other people's products onto television, the most powerful sales tool ever invented, in my view more powerful even than the Internet as a way of reaching out to people and getting them to open their pocketbooks *right now*.

So when you've found a likely product, what's the next step?

You need to establish a relationship with the manufacturer or owner of the product. Perhaps you'll start by saying, "I want to get your product on television and sell a ton of them for you."

If you're at a trade show, ask the people at the booth, "Has HSN been by?" "Do you have any arrangement with QVC?"

If the answers to both questions are no, you can step up to the line with, "I'll take it to HSN and QVC for you." Even if the product is already established in other markets, you're almost certain to raise interest. To any small-time inventor, entrepreneur, or businessperson, those words are magic.

You can seek to establish an arrangement with them in one of these ways:

- Become an agent for the product, receiving a royalty for each unit sold through deals you put together.
- Connect them with someone else you know who has access to television outlets or is already established at HSN and QVC, working out a finder's fee arrangement with the product inventor or company principal. ("Let's draw up an agreement that I'll be in for a couple of points if anything comes from this.")
- Arrange to buy quantities of the product at wholesale, and resell them.
- If you have capital behind you, you can share costs of rolling

out the product—though, as I've made clear elsewhere, this can run into the millions of dollars. For my company, joint partnerships are most often on a 50/50 or 40/60 split.

Of course you'll want your attorney to draw up the agreement; the handshake deals I made in my early days are a formula for disappointment and lawsuits.

Once the signatures are on paper, it's time for you to start making serious contacts with HSN and QVC.

✗ ALREADY ON THE AIR? ✗

Your opportunity for making money after you've discovered a product is by getting it on the Home Shopping Network or QVC, or in the best of all possible worlds, both of those shopping channels. (Incidentally, if you are an inventor or product manager—if the product is your own instead of someone else's—the basic strategy that follows will work for you as well, even though some of the specific steps will only apply when someone else owns the product.)

One red flag that will stop you in your tracks: if the listing in a catalog or a sign at a tradeshow says "As seen on TV," that's a sure sign that the shopping channels have already carried this product. You're too late—back to the research to find another product.

Even if that red-flag phrase doesn't appear, you still need to find out whether the shopping channels are already carrying the item or one like it. You can do this online, using QVC's "Product Search" feature; on the HSN website, it's called "Items Recently on Air."

✄ CONTACTING THE SHOPPING CHANNELS

If you find the path is clear, then the time has come to start contacting the shopping channels. They provide a process for doing this online—but they get so many inquiries that they don't respond very quickly. In fact, QVC tells you not to expect an answer in less than four to six weeks.

I much prefer a more direct approach, a phone call to one of their buyers. Of course, that's easy for me to say; I've brought both of these companies so much business over the years that they know me and will take my calls.

On the other hand, you've figured out by now that a large part of my success is because persistence is part of my nature. I don't have any doubt that I could call HSN or QVC, give a fictitious name, and talk my way into being connected to a buyer—maybe not on the first try, and maybe I'd have to come up with two or three different approaches before I found one that worked. And I would certainly need a product that's truly novel, not just some small twist on a too-familiar item.

If the product is as good as you think, and you are persuasive and effective in presenting it, you may indeed find yourself becoming the agent for the next million-dollar product.

Remember that when I was pioneering this business, I was groping my way, without the kind of guidance that you're finding in this book. Yet among the hundreds of products I've launched, more than twenty of them have had over $100 million in sales.

✒ TIPS AND TALES ✗

The challenge of finding new products has some different angles if you are already active in a particular industry. My first question is, how well are you keeping in touch with what's hot?

I recently met someone who had a clever product in the pet industry. This woman is young (probably midthirties) and a real go-getter, but when I talked to her about a hot new pet product I had run across, I discovered that she hadn't heard of it. Half a year later, as I write this, that product has become absolutely huge, probably the biggest gadget for pets to hit the marketplace in a decade.

At the time, this product was *the* big new thing in the marketplace, enjoying screaming sales. That she didn't know about it told me she wasn't keeping up with the goings-on in the industry in which she was trying to establish herself. If she had been keeping her ear to the ground, she might have discovered that product early on, and she might have been the person who took it to HSN and QVC.

You always need to be looking for the next big product.

I asked another person with a promising new product what international shows he had been to. "None," he told me.

Shows like MIPCOM can open your products to vastly increased sales. It you're not looking for overseas outlets, you're missing a great bet. Meanwhile, most of the other people in your field aren't going to the international marketplace shows either. When you go, you're getting the jump on all the others.

I'll end this recital with another experience I hope you will take encouragement from. Late one afternoon a few years ago, I was at Pepe's, a cantina near the Home Shopping Network campus in Tampa, socializing and schmoozing with some of the HSN people. I was introduced to one unfamiliar person in the crowd, a woman with a professional, buttoned-down look and an engaging manner. Her name was Karen Hyman. When I asked her what she did, she answered, "I'm in this boring business of selling coffee to companies. The most exciting thing in my day is 'Decaf or regular?'" She got the laugh she was looking for.

Just as I advise people to do within their circle of contacts, she checked in with me every now and then after that, always professional yet entertaining. One day when she called, I happened to be in the process of looking for someone to fill a staff position, so I offered her the job. She took it and worked for me about two years, then came to me and said, "It's time for me to start my own business." Using the knowledge, skills, and contacts she had acquired with me, she wanted to become a competitor. I gave her every encouragement and some leads to follow up.

Today, some seven years later, Karen has a *huge*, multi-million-dollar business, mostly selling products to QVC.

11

PICKING THE RIGHT PARTNERS

*It isn't the people you fire who will make
your life miserable; it's the people you don't fire.*

—Harvey Mackay, business executive and author

Picking the right partner is like getting married.

Sometimes we allow our instincts and emotions to rule, and congratulate ourselves afterward on the keenness of our instincts. Sometimes, instead, we live to regret that we did not allow ourselves to see a situation clearly.

An old adage conveys a part of this: "Marry in haste, repent at leisure." Some of my partnerships have turned out to be successful and highly profitable; some have turned out to be . . . well, let's just say they weren't the most pleasant experiences. Unlike some people we all know, who seem to keep picking the same type of inappropriate partner to date or marry, I at least haven't repeated my mistakes. Maybe that's because I've learned lessons from the successful experiences as well as the dreadful ones.

At National Media in 1994, I don't think anyone noticed that my three-year contract had expired. Under other circumstances, I would happily have stayed. But even though converting my options to stock had made me the number-two shareholder in the company, it felt pretty much the way it might have if I were working for a giant global corporation, running a small department under a division head who reported to a vice president, who reported to a group president, who reported to a far-off CEO. The capper came when I was ordered to cancel a show that was already in production. I like it better when I'm calling the shots. I would not extend my contract. It was time to go.

After I left, the company was sued for breach of contract over the show that had been cancelled. Apparently the company cancelled other shows that had been in early stages of production as well, because a series of lawsuits followed. It was like the old joke about "How do you create a one-hundred-million-dollar business? You start with a multi-hundred-million-dollar business." Four years later, National Media had folded.

Down the coast in Tampa, Home Shopping Network at that time was being run by Jerry Hogan, who had been brought in from Turner Broadcasting. We had been introduced by a mutual friend, Bob Swift. Several times when I was with Jerry, he had said, "When you leave National Media, talk to me." Not *if,* but *when.*

So Jerry was one of the first people I called. It turned out that he had been serious. Two months later I was living in St. Petersburg, just outside of Tampa. I had an equity partnership deal with Home Shopping, creating a new organization called HSN Direct, and the responsibility of putting them into the infomercial business. HSN is a more prosperous and powerful organization than many people realize, with a fifty-acre campus, one thousand employees, and $1.5 billion in annual sales.

Among my most rewarding and least troublesome partnership experiences was one from earlier in my career. After my first exposure to the MIPCOM conference and trade show in Cannes, during that horrifically intense period when I was trying to set up operations throughout Europe in six weeks, I was back again the following year. This time I wasn't looking for call center and fulfillment contractors but stations and networks from which I could purchase airtime. The staffers manning our booth told me that a lot of Japanese men kept hovering around it. Americans sometimes smile at how Japanese tourists always seem to have a camera hanging around the neck; these men were the same, and they were taking picture after picture of our booth. It seemed as if they were checking us out—but why?

Peter Brice, the WH Smith executive in England who I had convinced to let us buy their overnight dead airtime, had recently left Smith and approached me about working for us as a consultant. He had been impressed with how well we had performed in Europe, and I had been impressed by his business acumen and his contacts. One of the first things he did was join us for the MIPCOM show. He came to me and said, "The Japanese are from Mitsui, and they want to meet with you."

Mitsui, originally a banking company started in the 1600s,

has become a vast corporate giant; both Toshiba and Toyota are spin-offs from the mother company. It sounded as if they would be a powerhouse of a partner. And Brice was the guy who had sent them around to check us out.

The Mitsui people, I learned, were very eager to get into the business of selling products from America using the American method, the infomercial. At the time of my first meeting with their team, they were already convinced we were the group they wanted to work with. Their attitude was, "Let's do it. We want to be your partner."

We left Cannes at the end of the show with a handshake agreement to establish a partnership. After three months of due diligence on both sides and the usual lawyers' lawyering, the partnership documents were ready for signing.

Our infomercial and selling skills combined with Mitsui's savvy about the Japanese market, and their experience as importers and merchandisers, proved to be dynamite. In the very first year, the partnership did $80 million in sales, with a bottom line of $15 million in profits.

The secret of success here was that our Mitsui partners were truly committed to making the project successful and to making it very profitable.

In choosing partners, there is no substitute for commitment.

ARABIAN NIGHTS

When Sheikh Saleh Kamel of Saudi Arabia had his people get in touch with Home Shopping Network to say that they were looking for an experienced company to partner with to sell products on television, HSN replied that they were not interested in opening a live shopping channel in the Middle East. But they told him about their relationship with me.

How do you think you might respond if you were in a business like mine and were contacted by an Arab sheikh who owned five television channels beaming sports, movies, children's programming, and more to every one of the twenty Arabic-speaking countries throughout the region? You'd probably walk around with a gleam in your eye, right?

It wasn't long before I was on an airplane, stumbling off a day and a half later at the airport in the Red Sea port city of Jidda feeling completely done in, only to discover the incredibly distressing sight of what looked like a two-hour line at the Customs counters. I had been told to look for someone holding up a sign with my name on it, which I finally spotted at the far end of the mass of people. As politely as I could manage, I wedged and maneuvered my way to the front, where the man holding the sign locked a hand around my wrist and led me around the corner and into a private room. I was asked for my passport, I presented it, it was stamped . . . and we were on our way.

That was an impressive beginning. Apparently this sheikh was a very important man. When I asked my escort about the special service, he explained that Sheikh Saleh Kamel, in addition to his television channels and other businesses, owned the rights to several government functions. One of his organizations issued all the new drivers licenses and renewals. But it was a different one that gave him so much clout at the airport: the sheikh had the government contract for cleaning the toilets in all public buildings, including the airport! Well, okay, not exactly the clout I had imagined, but it had saved me a two-hour wait in line, and that was good enough for me.

I was driven by limo to the Sheraton Hotel, where I found I had to pass through a metal detector before being allowed to enter the lobby. I didn't care how modest the room was—I've stayed at many Holiday Inns in my life. I walked through the door to the room and could hardly believe my eyes. I was to be staying in a suite that looked as if it must occupy half of the entire floor. It had a living room, dining room, kitchen, and three bedrooms, each with its own bath. My mind was spinning.

My escort explained the schedule. Tomorrow I would rest and catch up on my sleep. In the evening I would have dinner with the sheikh on his 150-foot yacht. The following morning would be a business meeting, after which I would be taken on a tour of the city, followed by another dinner with the sheikh, this one at his home.

A message was beginning to sink in: I had come prepared to put on a dog-and-pony show about why my organization would be the best choice to help commercialize the sheikh's television operations. Now I could see that was the wrong tack. The *sheikh* was trying to impress *me*. It was time to rethink my strategy.

I'm not going to tell him how great we are, I thought. *I'm going to tell him I'm here to select a partner, and let him tell me why I should do business with him.*

Dinner aboard the yacht was as elegant as you could imagine, the big surprise being that this was not a dinner party for twelve or twenty people: I was the only guest. The sheikh was very open, not the reserved, unapproachable, holier-than-thou type I had imagined. Through the course of the evening, I learned that satellite dishes were illegal in Saudi Arabia. But there were millions of them, and the government didn't raise an eyebrow over the sheikh's channels broadcasting to people who were breaking the law by watching over a satellite dish hidden in the attic (or wherever Saudis hide their antennas). I also learned that the government would not object to the sheikh using my infomercials, dubbed into Arabic, to sell products to those same illegal viewers.

For the business meeting the following day, I showed up wearing my best suit, with an Hermès tie. I didn't notice until later that I had selected a tie with camels on it. The sheikh didn't comment—maybe he thought I was paying homage to his country.

He spent two hours working at convincing me why I should select him as my partner. Playing the role I had laid out for myself, I asked him, "Are you willing to make the commitment of money, time, and effort to support this?"

He told me, "I have to do this. I need a business for my son to run." The son was a man of about thirty-two who lived in a separate house on the sheikh's compound, a property that looked to be several hundred acres. The sheikh himself lived with his young second wife in what I was told was a $30 million house (and looked worth every bit that much). The first wife, to whom he was still married, lived in her own house elsewhere on the grounds.

When it came time to talk specifics, the sheikh had no problem putting up the full $5 million to launch the operation and was comfortable with my proposal of a 50/50 split on profits. It was not the kind of arrangement you make every day; obviously successful businesspeople in the oil-rich countries can afford different standards for doing business than the rest of us. I got back on the airplane to return home feeling that I had pulled off a coup, but knowing that this was going to be rewarding as well for the sheikh and for his son.

The first Arabic infomercials went on the air in 1996. On all the channels combined, we were beaming twenty hours a day of programming into millions of homes. In the first year, we sold $20 million worth of goods.

Then the operation started going downhill, for a reason you probably would not guess and I could not have anticipated: the son started putting a lot of family members on the payroll, and it was never clear to me that they were making much of a contribution to the business. He had fifty employees doing work that could have been done by thirty or fewer. The sheikh, bleeding $150 million a year from his television operations, finally announced to me, "We will stop giving away our programming free to everyone with a satellite dish. In thirty days, we go to a subscription model. The signal will be encrypted. It will cost a customer $20 a month to have it unscrambled."

Of course, many viewers weren't in a hurry to start paying for a service that until then had been free. In the television world, it's all about eyeballs—fewer eyeballs, fewer sales from infomercials.

I told the sheikh I didn't want to renew our contract. Though we parted amicably, it hurt to walk away from an operation that had registered gross sales of $25 million, but it was the only sensible decision. Today we sell to that region through distributors out of Cairo.

The lesson I learned was that in approaching any joint venture, no matter how prestigious and established your potential partner appears, you need to spell out the corporate governance in detail. Since my partner in this venture had deep pockets and was putting up all the money, I had allowed him to have operational control.

I have never again gone into a deal in which I did not have a voice in staffing decisions, financial decisions, and the other essential areas of running the business. At least I learned an important lesson:

Never give up complete operational control.

Happily, these bumpy joint ventures have been the exception. Most have been like my experience with a public company in the travel business, YTB Travel. When we started with them, they offered us 1 million shares of stock in exchange for producing an infomercial, which was then to be tailored to promote individual distributors in local cities—all on our own bankroll. In addition to the infomercials, we designed a marketing program for them and created a magazine.

Taking stock instead of cash can obviously be risky, but it was a great call in this case. They had 19,000 members when we began; that number increased to 150,000 once the infomercials started running. The stock went from $1 per share up and up and up. I sold off shares along the way, taking advantage of the climbing price, which reached a peak of $18 before sliding back a bit. The softening price didn't upset me, though. I had made many millions from the shares I sold.

What made the project such a pleasure was the time we spent with the company founder and leader, whom everyone calls Coach, a genuine guy and straight shooter.

I learned a lesson from this experience:

Always look to do business with people you would happily invite to Christmas dinner!

SILVER LINING

I first knew of the Franklin Mint in the years that my company and the Mint were both based in the Philadelphia area, and that company proved to be a gold mine for talent. The company was highly successful in the business of creating collectible coins and medallions, which they typically sold in sets. It was at one time owned by Linda and Stewart Resnick, a couple recognized as among the most successful private entrepreneurs in the country; under their management, the Mint became a billion-dollar business. They have since sold the company, and it's now being run by New York financier M. Moshe Malamud.

I started doing business with the Mint in 2007, producing an infomercial for their presidential coin sets, which generated enough enthusiasm that we did sales of over $10 million in the three months from the first television airings.

As I write this, Barack Obama was elected president two weeks ago. Here's an example of how fast my organization moves: we already have an Obama Presidential Coin project with the Mint, with television spots of one, two, three, four, and five minutes already airing in both English and Spanish.

Thanks to the overwhelming popularity of President Obama, this will go down in the annals of direct marketing as one of the most explosive campaigns in the history of our industry: the Obama Coins will shortly reach a sales level of 25,000 units a week.

By the time you read this, the campaign will have been launched in Canada, Latin America, and Europe.

To take advantage of sudden opportunities, maintain strong relationships with partner companies, and keep a lean organization staffed with people who can spring into action on a moment's notice.

12

WORKING WITH CELEBRITIES

Too much of a good thing can be wonderful.

—Mae West, actress

If you look down the list of the five hundred products we have promoted, you would quickly conclude that we are basically a marketing company for hard goods and gadgets—knives, ovens, blenders, fishing equipment, fitness and beauty products, and the like.

With these types of goods, product is king. You need a good product, a good story, and a good pitch. The pitch is the essence of the deal. We say, "Life's a pitch, and then they buy."

Using a celebrity in your advertising or promotion can draw huge attention to your product or service, but it comes at a cost—sometimes an emotional cost as well as a financial one. In my twenty-five years in business, and especially during those four years with Home Shopping Network, I've met and worked with Frank Abagnale (the *Catch Me If You Can* man), Frankie

Avalon, Connie Stevens, Vanna White, Sherman Helmsley, Suzanne Somers, Ivana Trump, Dick Clark, Phyllis Diller, George Foreman, Billy Mays, Victor Kiam, and more.

Celebrities usually get a hefty fee up front plus points on the back end—that is, a royalty based on sales. They only travel first class (often with at least one person from their staff, sometimes with their own hairdresser or makeup person, or both), they expect to be put up in a five-star hotel, usually in a suite, and to be driven everywhere in a limousine.

If you've seen a few infomercials, you know that on-camera hosts don't have to be celebrities. Tony Little wasn't on anyone's radar when we did his first infomercial in 1990, but he had a pitch, and it was powerful. So powerful, in fact, that the product, a home-exercise video called *Target Training*, sold 7 million copies, which is huge—enough to be the envy of most any small-business person or product manager.

That was followed by his Ab Isolator exercise device. We sold 7 million of those as well. Tony earned more than a dollar on each sale, and we made about the same.

Tony Little certainly was not a celebrity when we produced the shows; he became one as a result of them. And the pages of this book are filled with stories of other wildly successful products sold without any celebrity endorsement.

So when does a celebrity become worthwhile in promoting a product? My own answer is this:

A celebrity only becomes worthwhile when the celebrity is essentially the product.

In the early 1990s, when hardly any infomercials had been done for fitness products, a man named Bob Warden came in to see me with a device he had designed and patented that had two pedals, each cushioned by air; when you stepped on them alternately, you could exercise like going up an unending flight of stairs.

You could go to a gym and do something very similar using a machine that carried a price tag in the neighborhood of $3,000 to $5,000. The home product, manufactured in quantity, could sell for around $95. I saw this as an item that justified shooting a high-end infomercial, and one that would benefit from featuring a sports celebrity. One of the names at the top of my list was Bruce Jenner. Although he had earned his Olympic gold medal in the decathlon more than a decade earlier, he was still a celebrated national hero.

These days, thanks to the Internet, it's fairly easy to find out who represents a celebrity. Back then it was more of a challenge, and, in fact, I found my way to him through an unexpected backdoor channel. I had made contact with Jack Kirby, a talented young man, formerly a producer for *CBS Morning News*, who had recently set up his own production company in Los Angeles. When I mentioned Jenner's name to him, Jack said he got his hair done at a salon on the Sunset Strip by a guy who also did the hair of Bruce's wife, Kris. Jack talked to the stylist for me, who said he would relay the request if I would be willing to consider a product idea he had for an infomercial. Of course I agreed. (His product idea was a winner, a home hair product that we called the Jet Aire YES Curler and successfully sold through an infomercial that featured him as host.)

Bruce's wife had previously been married to Robert Kardashian, famous for being a lead attorney on the O. J. Simpson defense team. When I showed the Stair Climber to Bruce and Kris, they flipped over it and were enthusiastic about appearing in the infomercial. It would be their first infomercial, and the first product Bruce had endorsed since the Olympics. They had such a resounding success with the Stair Climber that they went on to do shows selling two other fitness products, the Power Walk, and the Minimax Gym. All together, Bruce and Kris have accounted for sales of some half a billion dollars.

The Jenner/Kardashian clan turned out to be naturals on camera, with another of the family joining our list of infomercial celebrity hosts when Kris's daughter Kim Kardashian worked with us in 2005 on the show for the Pressa Bella steam iron. It wasn't long before Bruce, Kris, Kim, and the rest of the clan could be seen weekly on the E! channel in their own popular TV reality show, *Keeping Up with the Kardashians*.

WOLFMAN

Celebrities can make a product, but they can also break the bank of your company.

Our first celebrity infomercial was a show we did in 1988

with Wolfman Jack, who back then was the hottest, most famous radio disk jockey in the country. By that time we were regularly doing our taping in front of a live studio audience. It wasn't like gathering an audience for a taping of *Friends* or *The Tonight Show*; for popular shows like those, people write months in advance or stand in line for a few hours for tickets. For an infomercial audience, you promise people a fee (today it's typically around $100) plus a catered lunch if they will sit in your studio for eight hours of taping. So two hundred warm bodies can set you back $20,000.

I had something much bigger in mind for the Wolfman Jack taping. I wanted it to be like what they used to call a sock hop, a large room crowded with people dancing feverishly to the music. I wanted a thousand people, which meant a budget item of $100,000 just for the audience. As I recall, we were paying Wolfman $20,000 up front to do the deal. Add the fee for his agent, plus airfares, plus the cost of production, and we were over $200,000 even before the cost of the audience.

To make this pay off, we put Wolfman on all the local TV interview shows, and all the local radio stations, two days before the event. On each show, we had them announce, "Wolfman is in town, and there are a limited number of free tickets that Wolfman is personally going to give away to the first callers." We had the interviewers all pumped up over this, so they were adding things like, "You've got to call in right away because these tickets are going to go fast."

The day of the taping, the thousand people with tickets

showed up, but so did five hundred additional people burning to see Wolfman in person. It turned out great for us because we saved $100,000 by not paying those people to be there. But it was great for them, as well, because so many of them got one-on-one face time with the phenom, Wolfman.

What was the product all this fuss was about? It had started out just to be a collection of rock-and-roll oldies. Then we came up with the idea of seeing if we could tie in a celebrity. Wolfman Jack was turned on by the concept, I suppose because he liked the additional publicity he would get, and he was satisfied with the fee we offered. We told him to come up with the top 100 songs of all time in rock-and-roll history. He started with 1,500 of his favorites, whittled it down to 500, and managed to get it down to 200. At that point he called me and said, "Kevin, there's no way I can get it down to a hundred."

I talked it over with my people who were handling the project, called him back and said, "Okay, we'll let you go to 150."

When he showed up to close the deal, he told me that he had been able to get it down to 151, but couldn't get it down any further. He said they were the songs that he listened to with breakfast in the morning and when he was having a couple of beers before going to bed. They were his all-time favorites. "This," he said, "is Wolfman's private collection."

The story of Wolfman not being able to get the number down below 151 was, of course, something we played up heavily in the infomercial and the marketing for the collection.

I've always been a risk taker. To some degree, an entrepreneur who wants to be something more than just a modest success has to take risks. Fortunately, my batting average hasn't been too shabby.

Wolfman Jack was definitely a risk. Up until then, we had never spent more than $40,000 on any one show. The $200,000 budget on this one had me holding my breath. But we had been getting a little push-back from some of the stations on the quality of our shows; what had been acceptable in the pioneer days of the industry was starting to be seen as a little shabby. Unlike the experience with Earl Greenberg's efforts, by this time the stations were saying, "Give us better-looking shows; we'll give you better time slots." We were going to have to start moving upstream with our budgets, and "a rock-and-roll favorites" product turned out to be a great place to begin.

The Wolfman show turned out to open an unexpected door for me later on. In 1990, I read about an upcoming huge music event in New York at which Malcolm Forbes, the publisher of *Forbes* magazine, was going to be speaking. I got in touch with the organizers to see if I could cadge an invitation. Later a report made its way back to me that when they received my request, someone wanted to know, "Who is this Harrington?" The answer she got was, "He's the guy who did the first-ever music infomercial." The Wolfman Jack show had unexpectedly given me credibility in the music business.

At the event, the people who had made it possible for me to be there introduced me to Forbes. He told me, "I don't know much about your industry, but I've seen your music infomercial."

We chatted for a bit, and then he said, "I'm going out of the country for about ten days. When I get back, I want to get together because I have some thoughts on some products that you might be able to help us sell with infomercials."

Two days later, a letter landed on my desk from Mr. Forbes's secretary, confirming that he wanted to meet with me once he was back from his trip. Although a heart attack took his life just after his return, the experience was an eye-opener. From it I gained the sense of "I can do anything with anybody."

My pursuit of Donald Trump came shortly after. I would never again think someone was too big or too important to pursue—if I had something of value to offer them.

Heroine

For anybody who will ever consider using a celebrity for a commercial, here is a cautionary tale. Sometimes talent isn't enough.

We signed up to do an infomercial for a company that had a skin-care line. They said they wanted to shoot in Baden-Baden, Germany, famed for its healthy spring waters, a town with such a long history that it still has the remnants of ancient Roman baths.

As their on-camera spokesperson, the client wanted to use an actress then appearing on one of the most popular prime-time soap operas in the history of television. I understood the logic. The media often referred to her as "the most beautiful woman on television" and even "the world's number-one sex symbol." For promoting a skin-care product, she seemed like a natural choice.

The deal we were able to work out included a $50,000 payment up front, plus flying the actress, her personal assistant, and her hairstylist to the shoot in Germany, and a provision that she could rent her "lucky dress" to wear on camera. We sent a ton of samples of the products for her to start trying, so she could satisfy herself that they really worked.

She was impossible from the moment she arrived in Germany. She complained about the airline flight, she complained about the limousine, she complained about the hotel. Nothing was good enough.

The next morning, she came down in a snit. She had read the script and didn't like that either. She said, "I'm the *host*. I'm not endorsing the f—ing product." She would agree to be interviewed, she said, "But I won't say I have ever used the product."

We managed to get an infomercial in the can, but it was full of compromises. Before we were done, she had a knock-down-drag-out with her personal assistant, who had only been working for her for a month. The assistant quit and flew back to the States. She called our offices a week later to say, "By the way, when you get the bill for $4,000 for renting her 'lucky dress,' don't pay it. She didn't rent it—that's a dress she owns."

This was the only infomercial we've ever done that never aired.

The lesson I learned, painfully, from this outlandish experience is that it's not enough to ship the product to the celebrity. Ever since that fiasco, our celebrity contracts have specifically stated that the person needs to experience the product and satisfy himself or herself that it lives up to the claims. This is a matter of ethics, but it's also a matter of believability: you want your host to speak from the heart, promoting the product not just because that's what the script says but because he or she is personally convinced. If your celebrity doesn't have passion about the product, don't expect the campaign to be a success.

If I had had those terms in our contract with the television actress, I could have saved a great deal of aggravation, and close to $300,000.

The Fascinating Man

If you ever saw the movie *Catch Me If You Can,* you probably can't forget this true story of a teenager who managed to pass himself off as an airline pilot, a lawyer, and even a doctor heading an emergency room staff, and who figured out how to create such authentic-looking checks that banks and hotels never spotted them as phony.

The story was so improbable and dazzling that the movie project drew some of Hollywood's most impressive talents: Spielberg as director, Tom Hanks as the FBI agent leading the search, and Leonardo DiCaprio as the central character, Frank Abagnale Jr.

Abagnale has since then carved a career for himself as a highly respected consultant to the FBI, banks, and businesses and as a successful businessman in his own right. If you had the chance to meet him, you might be expecting to find a dapper, polished, self-assured man. You'd be on the nose.

When I worked out a deal to partner with the Affinion Group on an identity-theft protection program called "Total Guard," the arrangements included the services of Frank Abagnale to appear as the host of the infomercial. He showed up at our studios in Fort Lauderdale right on time, at 7 AM, looking wide-awake though a little reserved, almost shy. But as soon as he stepped in front of the camera, the reserve dropped away and he sprang to life, professional and engaging.

As an infomercial host, Frank became an overnight star. The product is valuable and impressive in its own right; with Frank Abagnale presenting and explaining it, sales boomed from the very first.

I think I've never met so fascinating a man.

THE ROLLING STONES

Sometimes opportunities pop out of nowhere. In 1989 I stumbled on a piece of intriguing information: a man named

Dennie Somach owned the rights to the original artwork created for the sleeves of the LP recordings of the early albums by the Beatles, the Rolling Stones, and others. In the days before audiotapes and CDs, the cover designs for those old albums were works of art. If I could make a deal to sell reproductions through an infomercial, I thought it would prove to be lucrative for me and for Somach.

We worked out an arrangement for selling lithographs of the designs as large, framed pieces of art, and I negotiated a deal for exclusive television rights, initially for the Rolling Stones. We would offer a version that included the handwritten signatures of Mick Jagger and the rest of the band for somewhere between $2,000 and $10,000, depending on how popular the album had been, and another version with signatures reproduced on the lithograph for $195.

Of course, I wanted to use footage of the Stones in concert for the infomercial. The price I was quoted by their licensing people floored me. Yes, they'd be happy to let me have the footage, for $250,000.

I thought that killed the project.

As it happened, though, the local Tampa/St. Petersburg Museum of Science and Industry was just then doing national distribution of an IMAX movie of the Stones. On television, they were running commercials for the film that included footage of the Stones in concert. I sat down with the Museum's people and told them about my project, explaining that I wanted to put a tag inside our show promoting their movie in exchange for the right to use footage from their commercial.

It seemed to them like great advertising that wouldn't cost them anything. And that's how I landed rights to the Stones' concert footage free of charge. What's more, the Museum offered to sell our lithographs in the IMAX theatres for a share of the sales.

We sold millions of dollars worth of those lithographs. But you can never tell who's going to be watching your infomercials. One of the Stones happened to catch a showing one night and the next day called their agent to ask what the deal was. The situation became quite sticky until I managed to work things out so everyone was happy.

To me, the experience just proved that *everybody* watches an infomercial every now and then.

SASSOON

Certainly one of the most beautiful women I've ever worked with is the extraordinary Beverly Sassoon. I met her when she was already divorced from her husband Vidal, the famed hairstylist and creator of a successful line of hair products. She had unfortunately lost her source of income. (Her divorce settlement provided her with a very ample cash flow, with the proviso that the payments would continue until she remarried; on a trip to Spain, she awoke one morning to learn that she had, the night before, married a bullfighter. The marriage was annulled, but it didn't matter that it had been a mistake: Vidal was off the hook, and Beverly's income stopped.)

I thought Vidal's fame all but guaranteed that a line of Beverly Sassoon beauty products would be a can't-miss winner, and I happily hired Beverly to head up a new Beauty Division for us. We created cosmetics, nail polish, and even pet shampoo and vitamins.

I tried for two years to make a success of the line. Beverly was bright and engaging and a pleasure to have around, but she was no entrepreneur. The Sassoon name wasn't enough. We didn't lose money on the effort, but we didn't make any to speak of, either.

This proved to be another example of the truism that it almost always takes more than a celebrity name to bring success.

Mr. President

Bill Clinton, I discovered, was a man willing to go out hunting for ideas for improving the country. In 1996 I was one of eight entrepreneurs invited to have a private dinner with the president.

During dinner, the conversation was just small talk. After we were through, the president said, "Okay, I'd like to hear some ideas." One man raised the issue of health care; Clinton gave him a straight political answer, a stock response that could have been right out of a political speech. Another talked about the

Gulf War; again, a straight political response.

The president said, "This is the shit I get all day long from reporters and critics. I brought you together to hear something fresh. Who's got something fresh?"

I said, "Mr. President, the government has so many assets. There must be tons of stuff that's not needed anymore. Instead of talking about cutting budgets, here's a way of increasing revenues." He seemed to be paying attention now, so I went on. "Public Broadcasting goes dark at midnight. Why not take those dark hours from midnight to 6:00 AM to sell unwanted government assets."

"That's a really interesting idea," he said. "I'd like you to give me a white paper on that."

I didn't know what a white paper was, but of course I said, "Absolutely!"

At the end of the evening, as the group was breaking up, the president said to me, "Can I talk to you privately?"

He wanted more details of what I had been suggesting. The army had developed a special new kind of boot for the ground forces in the Gulf War. I offered the idea of having additional quantities manufactured and using an infomercial to sell them to the American working man, and I offered a couple of additional thoughts along the same lines.

The president thanked me, said good night, and started out. One of his aides lagged behind for a moment to get my business card. But he said, "Don't waste too much time on this. Don't expect anything to happen. It's politics."

I did send a carefully crafted letter with a group of ideas spelled out in some detail. The aide was right. Other than getting a nice letter back from the president, I never heard anything further about it.

THE HILTON MYSTIQUE

I can't think of any better example to illustrate the power of celebrity than Kathy and Paris Hilton. Both of them have beauty products on the market, and Kathy's infomercials are handled by us. Home Shopping Network has 220 beauty brands, mostly celebrity driven. They have so many that they were putting the word out, "Don't bring us another skin-care product." But the Hilton name is magic; HSN's answer was *yes!*

Kathy came into my life in 2006, when the agent representing her called to ask, "Would you be interested in purchasing a class-three license from Kathy Hilton?" Translation: Did I want to acquire the exclusive rights to market hair, makeup, skin-care, and fragrance products that would be created, bearing her name.

There aren't many names more promotable these days than Hilton. I leaped at the chance. I got that brand for seven figures.

Kathy Hilton is not only a pleasant, sweet person, she's also a surprisingly good businesswoman. She loves to tell the story of how a customer would come into her retail store in Beverly Hills, buy $100 worth of goods, and be happily ready to leave, when Kathy would sweep up to her and offer to show some other items that she was sure would please. Often the customer would leave a while later with another $1,000 of purchases.

From the first time I had dinner together with her and her husband, Rick, she made it a point to put me at ease. She would come with a bag of products to show, rubbing creams on my hands and telling me, "This is what I use; this is what Paris uses." Her approach was so unaffected that it blew me away. I thought, *Finally—a celebrity who knows how to sell!*

For the perfume line, Kathy picked out flowers that she liked and sent them to the perfume maker, telling him, "This is the scent I want."

The timing of Kathy's product introduction couldn't have been better: daughter Paris was just then scheduled to launch her new perfume, Can Can, at the famous Selfridges department store on Oxford Street in London. I knew there would be a huge mob of paparazzi, and indeed there was—there must have been more than a hundred media people. I had hired my own film crew and sent them out with specific instructions on what I wanted them to photograph.

Kathy, Rick, and I arrived in a limo, and the cameras were clicking away as we got out and stepped onto the red carpet. I slipped to the side, leaving the handsome Rick and my gorgeous product-partner Kathy to parade for the paparazzi. The timing worked out exactly as I had planned. The two of them had been basking in the limelight for several minutes when another limo pulled up, and out stepped their daughter Paris. The three Hiltons hugged and fussed over each other while the paparazzi clicked away furiously. Meanwhile, my camera team was capturing the Hiltons but focusing even more on the clamor and furor of the frenetic paparazzi—footage that I knew would play great in Kathy's infomercial.

We launched Kathy's new product that very night on the Ideal channel in the United Kingdom, featuring a ton of footage of Kathy, Paris, and the paparazzi. And more: the paparazzi knew Kathy's schedule. They knew that we were going to be showing up at the studios of Ideal that night, and a flock of them were gathered when we arrived. Ideal had two of their own camera crews outside, standing by at the ready.

Our arrival triggered a media frenzy. Meanwhile, Ideal interrupted their programming and went live with the arrival, while their announcer excitedly advised the audience to "stay tuned because Kathy Hilton is here, and you're going to be seeing the world launch of Kathy's products and perfumes coming up in the next hour."

Rick, Kathy, Paris, and I met for a late dinner that night at the celebrity-favorite Japanese restaurant Nobu, and I got to meet the famous chef in person when he joined us at the table for the meal—something he certainly wouldn't have done if I had been dining at his restaurant on my own.

At the end of the night, when we got back into the limousine and drove away, a flock of paparazzi actually pursued us. It was like something out of a movie.

What a far cry from our earliest infomercials, those whole-night shoots on a kitchen set in the back of a supermarket! And it was a good example of the mileage you can get with a celebrity who is a big enough star to draw the paparazzi.

For me it was another eye-opener. The amount of publicity was enormous, with newspaper and magazine headlines trumpeting, "Mother and daughter launch their products here." Even the stately *Times of London* covered the story. The free publicity we got was worth millions.

It takes a powerfully large budget to be able to afford a celebrity like Kathy Hilton—but the impact can be tremendous. Yet you only get value from a celebrity if you use the full power of what they bring to the table.

Still, my bottom-line message on the subject of celebrities is:

If the product is really strong, you don't need a celebrity.

Hulk Hogan and wrestler Brian Knobs with Kevin Harrington at a Tampa Bay Rays baseball game in 2009.

Tony Little with the Ab Isolator, one of the biggest infomercial successes with over $200 million in sales.

Billy Mays, one of the most successful infomercial hosts in the history of the business, with top infomercial producer Anthony Sullivan and Kevin.

Tim Harrington, Kathy Hilton, and Kevin in 2008, on the set for the Kathy Hilton beauty products infomercials aired in the U.S., Canada, and Europe.

Wife (Crystal) and Kevin with Michelle Obama at a political fund-raiser in 2008.

Kevin Harrington with President Bill Clinton at a private dinner for a few entrepreneurs, in 1996.

Kevin with Morty Moosavi, long-time distributor for international sales of infomercial TV products, currently focusing on selling to Europe and the Middle East.

Kevin with popular European and American infomercial pitchman John Parkin (known as "the Man with the Bowtie). Recognized for his various household and auto-polishing products, Parkin achieved fame when he lit a car on fire in an infomercial for car wax (circa late eighties/early nineties).

Kevin Harrington sitting at the actual desk of inventor Thomas Edison at the Invention Incubator Facility located in Ashbury Park, New Jersey (2002).

Kevin with popular TV selling hosts, Anthony Sullivan (Sully) and Billy Mays, the stars of the TV program *Pitchman*, at the premiere launch party in 2009.

Kevin with celebrity Joan Rivers at Kevin's home in St. Petersburg, Florida in 2009.

Actress Hunter Tylo flanked by brothers Tim and Kevin Harrington at the Tampa Bay "Lightning" hockey game on the award-winning evening of their Stanley Cup Victory, 2004.

Kevin, age 11, at the wheelbarrow he used as the stepping-stone to begin his entrepreneurial career, with baby brother Tim.

Malcolm Forbes with Kevin at a music industry function, discussing a future project together shortly before Forbes' death in 1990.

The Great Wok of China, which sold more than 3 million units in 1988, was one of Kevin's first pioneering infomercials.

The award-winning "Q" Grill, acknowledged for its unique design, was a consistent big seller through infomercal marketing to TV-viewing audiences worldwide.

Kevin chose renowned radio DJ and rock 'n' roll enthusiast "Wolfman Jack," a high profile DJ in the 1950s and 1960s, to compile the greatest hits of the decades, and created the first televised music infomercial, which went on to sell millions of units in the late 1980s.

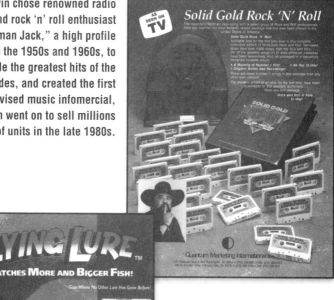

The Original "Flying Lure," which Kevin made popular with TV sales of over 500 million lures in the 1990s, was the #1 infomercial of its kind.

The Blade infomercial, starring celeb host Arnold Morris, sold millions of products in the late 1980s, leading Kevin to the acquisition of the rights to sell the popular Ginsu Knife.

EPILOGUE

At an industry convention in the late summer of 2008, a woman sought me out, explaining that several people had mentioned my name. She told me she was with Mark Burnett Productions and that Burnett was the guy who had created the shows *The Survivor* and *The Apprentice*—which, of course, I already knew. She said Burnett was now gearing up to do a show that would be something like *American Idol*, except that instead of people showing off their singing talents, this show would have people showing off their product ideas and their new-business concepts.

She wanted to know if I would be interested in being considered as a panelist for the show. I wasn't sure this was really something I wanted to spend my time doing. On the other hand, I have obviously always been drawn by new challenges. So, I told her I'd be willing to be considered. She asked me to put together some clips of myself doing television interviews and ship them to the Burnett offices in California. I put together a reel, and included, among others, an appearance on CNN and an occasion when I was on Donny Deutsch's show, and he described me in highly flattering terms, such as "industry guru."

A couple of weeks later, the woman called to say that Mark Burnett wanted to talk to me and asked if I would be willing to fly to Los Angeles—at my own expense. I admit I was curious to meet the man who was one of the founders of reality television, which is how I later I came to be sitting in a conference room at the company's offices not far from the Santa Monica beach.

The room had quite a little crowd assembled to talk to me, but no Mark Burnett. The show was to be called *Shark Tank,* loosely following the format of a show called *Dragon's Den* that had originated in Asia, with a North American version that had been drawing good audiences in Canada for four seasons.

The concept wasn't what you might expect. Unlike *American Idol, Shark Tank* contestants would not be vying to be the last person standing at the end of the season. Rather, each offering would be weighed on its own merits. Each one that looked as if it offered significant promise as a business prospect would then become the target of a "bidding war" among the panelists. . . . *I'll offer a quarter of a million dollars for twenty-five percent of the company* and so on.

Each contestant would have a half hour or an hour to make his presentation on video, which would then be edited down to around five minutes of the most compelling parts, which would then be assembled into an episode of the show.

I spent about an hour of back-and-forth with the group, part of the time with the team explaining the concepts to me, and part of the time with what I took to be something of a trial by fire, in which the people took turns shooting questions at me, some of the questions designed to make me squirm so they could see how I might handle myself under pressure.

And then Mark Burnett himself came into the room. He looked younger than I expected, and extremely fit, which is not surprising given that he was once in the British Armed Forces.

Burnett and I hit it off immediately. He told me he had been in telemarketing in England and had found it to be a rough-and-tumble industry with a lot of flaky people. Because of that, he said, he had big respect for people who had weathered the storm and made a success of it.

Then he said, "Kevin, as good as you are, I've only screened the one piece of tape you sent of the Deutsch show. Well, Deutsch is very powerful, he carries the show, but it didn't let me see who *you* are. There was nothing in it that showed me what you could do as a *Shark Tank* panelist. Would you mind if I send you in the other room to do a screen test?"

A screen test! Thinking back to that moment, I can't help chuckling at the idea. I'm a businessman. I thought a screen test was just something they did for an actor who was up for an important role in a movie or to be the star of a television series.

Still, I'm not easily phased. I said, "Sure."

Burnett shook my hand, I was escorted out of the room and led, not to a studio, but to a very professional makeup lady who spent twenty minutes fussing over my appearance.

The screen test lasted for more than an hour, with several of the same people from the earlier meeting firing away at me, mostly taking turns as if they were role playing as an inventor. Up front, they had told me, "We're not looking for you to just pat the guy on the back."

They wanted to see I would come up with challenging, probing, analytical questions. Could I analyze a presentation quickly, and then explain what appealed to me about the proposition and what I didn't like. And I assumed they wanted to see whether I could be tough when the situation called for it.

"Pretend I just presented a product you didn't like. What are you going to say?" In other words, could I be hard-nosed or amusing with somebody who has a lousy product? I felt I was projecting, getting powerful with my voice—just as I do with my own people when I have to.

At end of shoot, they seemed impressed with my performance. My piece would be edited and sent to ABC, they said.

Before leaving, I told them, "I've been a shark for twenty-five years. This is what I do every day—pick the winners and get rid of the losers"

I flew home convinced that this was something that would be a great lark, something I would get a huge kick out of. I knew I wouldn't hear immediately. I also knew that waiting was going to have me in a state of suspense.

Welcome to Hollywood. Weeks went by with no word. *Weeks.* Then one day when I had almost forgotten about Burnett and his *Shark Tank,* the phone call came, "You've been picked to be a shark. Congratulations."

Shooting the pilot would require me to be in Los Angeles for a full week. This time all expenses were paid for by Burnett's company—business-class air travel, a plush room at the Sofitel on Beverly Boulevard, a separate limo for each of the panelists, and a separate dressing room for each of us.

My fellow panelists turned out to be a group of impressive, highly accomplished people. Two were veterans from the Canadian version of the show, two others were people with big high-tech success stories, one was lady who is a powerhouse in real estate, and another guy was a hip-hop retail specialist. And then there was a billionaire, who I think must have been included as the "Simon Cowell" of the panel.

For four days in a row, we were picked up at 7 AM, spent the day on a sound stage at the CBS Radford Studios, and our limos dropped us off back to the hotel, dead tired, as late as 11 PM. We listened to a couple of dozen presentations, many of them eye-openers, as fascinating as the people pitching them to us.

The production techniques were almost as mind-boggling as the presentations. I'm used to shooting infomercials with four cameras rolling simultaneously. The *Shark Tank* pilots were shot with *sixteen* cameras.

The Burnett people liked the idea of tagging me as "the King of Infomercials," the label that appears on the cover of this book. It became the way I was identified in the pilot shows, as well.

As I write this, in March 2009, I know that Mark Burnett is

very pleased with the final version of *Shark Tank* that was delivered to the network for review. But it's still too early to know if ABC will find a place for the show in the summer schedule, and whether you will be able to get to know me in a different way by seeing me once a week on network television.

If so, I hope you have as much pleasure watching *Shark Tank* as I have had in helping the show become a reality.

A TIP OF THE HAT

You know by now that I believe very strongly in the value of connecting with other people who share similar business problems and challenges, and with people who have already walked some of the paths you are now walking.

I want to put in a blatant plug for an organization I've mentioned earlier in these pages: the Entrepreneurs Organization, EO. Recall that I was one of the founding members when Verne Harnish started the group as YEO, aimed at bringing together young business owners and entrepreneurs who were already highly successful. Just recently I've had a series of personal experiences that demonstrate how valuable this organization can be.

I hadn't been active in EO for some time, partly because there was no longer a chapter in Tampa. With a nudge from the organization's headquarters, I set out to launch a new local chapter by inviting fifty or so entrepreneurs to my home in St. Petersburg.

That gathering did bring enough sign-ups to launch an EO chapter, but it also lived up to its purpose by bringing me into contact with several people I will likely be doing business with. In fact, in two cases, I began doing business with these folks within weeks of meeting them. One of them was an old contact I hadn't seen in quite some time, Greg Stemm, a slender, bearded man who looks as if he might have been stranded on an island for years. The owner of Odyssey Shipwreck Marine Co., Greg told me they had found a shipwreck off the coast of Spain and recovered $500 million worth of old coins. He talked to me about whether an infomercial would be an effective way to sell the coins. I agreed it would, and as I write, we're moving ahead with plans to do that.

There's a man in Tampa by the name of Ken Lucci who runs a limo service and provides limos for my company. When I told him about the Entrepreneurs Organization, he said, "Yes, I guess you could call me an entrepreneur. But I don't think I'm the kind of entrepreneur you're looking for." I invited him to attend that night, where he got into a conversation with someone from Home Shopping Network who asked Ken to come in and talk to them about providing their limo service. He did. He called me afterward and said, "Kevin, you won't believe this. I picked up their account. And I'm not even a member of the EO yet. How do I join?" HSN could become one of his biggest accounts.

In another case, Amber McConklin, a real go-getter of a woman, became an EO member after the session at my house and was grateful for the mentoring she received from me and from some of the other members. Her product category is one that I have never done an infomercial for, but our conversations have led in that direction, and it's likely that we will be working together.

Amber struck me as typical of people who are drawn to an organization like EO, the kind of people who have a thirst for new knowledge and at the same time are ready to do anything they can for a fellow member.

And then there was Nick Freedman, a young EO member who had just recently moved to Tampa from Washington, D.C. He called one of the local members to explain the help he was looking for, that man sent out a memo, and several of us met with Nick for lunch. Though only twenty-something, with a fresh-faced look, Nick came across as a powerful self-starter, reminding me of myself at his age.

Nick had started a business, College Hunks Hauling Junk, providing pickup of junk, debris, and unwanted documents from home and office. As an inducement to clients, he trumpets that he's providing work for local college students, and the company uses the slogan "Let tomorrow's leaders haul your junk today."

What impressed me most was that Nick had already sold thirteen franchises. Through EO, he now has experienced advisers to ask for guidance and a roster of people in a variety of fields he can call on.

From the very beginnings, the emphasis of the organization has been on learning from others and making yourself available to answer questions or provide guidance when a fellow member calls on you for help. There is a sincerity and dedication in many of the people who join this group that make it a pleasure to be in their company. And I always know that anywhere in the country or the world I go, I can find EO members to offer solutions to any problem that may come up.

I'm thankful to EO and unreservedly recommend the organization to anyone in business who wants to benefit from the wisdom and experience of his or her peers.

EO is now in forty-three countries with over 6,000 members.

ACKNOWLEDGMENTS

From Kevin Harrington

My thoughts for acknowledgements turn first to my mother. She lived to see this no-college-degree son achieve a degree of success she could never have imagined. I can only wish she were still alive to be able to read this book; she would have been so proud. She would have been pleased, too, that lately I have found myself returning to the religion that meant so much to her. Her tombstone reflects how much she meant to our father, identifying her as "Charlie's Angel." I think of her as Kevin's Angel as well. I talk to her in my prayers and thank her for still being with me.

As you may remember from the first chapter of this book, it was from my father that I inherited and acquired my entrepreneurial spirit, and I'm ever thankful for his pushing me at early age to become entrepreneurial. I'm happy to report that he is now eighty-seven and still tough as nails. People speak of me as tough, loyal, and willing to work in the trenches. That description pleases me, and they are all qualities I got from my dad. Even more, I learned from him how to deal with the toughest times—and would not be where I am today without that quality.

I can also say that I wouldn't be where I am today without my brother Tim, now my full partner in the business. Tim is the guy who keeps everything running, makes sure we're doing the right deals, and hammers out the terms, leaving me able to do the freewheeling and stay focused on the business side of the business that has made everything possible. Sometimes it's easy to be the front guy saying yes, but I couldn't do it without Tim there to make it all happen.

My greatest share of appreciation goes to my treasure—my wife, Crystal. From the time we met over five years ago, her being in my life has happily changed me from a bachelor to a family man and given me a renewed focus of continuing to build the business while at the same time honoring family values and thinking about my personal future. Even more, she's not a treasure just to me alone. These days, my long-time friends are calling on her when they're having a problem. She has become the level-headed, calming advice-giver for everyone with a problem. People have said about me that I have a "Ready, Fire, Aim" mentality. Crystal has turned that into "Ready, Aim, Fire." I'm blessed to have her in my life.

Since this is my first book, I don't know what other book agents are like, but I can't imagine they come any better than Bill Gladstone. If I hadn't been lucky enough to find him, I'm sure the idea of doing this book would still be a dream. He is the man who has made it possible.

I'm grateful as well to Peter Vegso and Tom Sand at Health Communications, Inc., who had the vision even in a tight economy to see the potential in telling the story of how the infomercial came to be.

Finally and most of all, I want to acknowledge the remarkable talents of my coauthor, Bill Simon. It's been an amazing experience for me to see our many conversations turned one by one into flowing language that captures not only the trials, tribulations, and triumphs of my story, but the emotional content of each incident. I hope one day that I will do another book so I can again enjoy the rich experience of working with him.

From Bill Simon

I wish my darling wife, Arynne, had been able to read this manuscript before it was published. Any writer is blessed to have as tough and demanding a critic at his shoulder. Perhaps by the time my next book and next screenplay are taking shape, a few months from now, I'll have her sharp eye back on duty to goad me on and ensure the work meets her demanding standards.

But I can as always count on the caring attention of the rest of my closest family—Victoria, David, Sheldon, Merrilee, and grandchildren Vincent and Elena Bermont.

Kevin Harrington ranks as one of the most dynamic, energetic, life-force-at-the-max coauthors I've ever been fortunate enough to work with. How he found the time for this project in the midst of his busy career is a mystery I will never solve. During the time we worked together, he got married to his stunning and engaging Crystal, was into and out of major deals, bought ownership of an entire production studio, and graciously allowed his home to be used for major charity events that interrupted his life, all while this manuscript was in progress. In my view, Kevin ranks as a superstar of the business world and a superstar as a host and friend.

Paula Kaye has been a faithful support in helping me keep grounded, encouraging me with walks along the beach, dragging me to the gym, and keeping my brain swept clear of cobwebs. I will be grateful forever.

Evan Z has become a great bouncing-board and a lift to the spirits, a new friend and a true friend, and I hope a friend for always.

My literary agent, Bill Gladstone, continues to amaze by finding projects for me that are challenging, fascinating, and usually entirely different from anything I've done before. It certainly helps that he has such an impressive, remarkable circle of contacts and friends. And his efficient staff at Waterside Productions, including agent Ming Russell and money-lady Maureen Maloney, assure that my creative and financial matters are well looked after.

Finally, as in the past, I pay respects to the memory of my parents, but most especially my dad, who painstakingly corrected my grammar (even including letters home from summer camp, returned with errors marked); to television writer Sy Salkowitz, who breathed life into my career as a film writer; and to Cornell professor Lawrence Burkmyer, who encouraged me to pursue the career path that led me to where I am today. All live in my memory and continue to inspire.

POSTSCRIPT

It's said that even in places in the world where some people talk about the United States as the enemy and feel a degree of hatred toward this country, many of those same people still burn with a desire to come here, settle, and enjoy the benefits of our freedoms and way of life.

Why is that?

In large part I believe it's because this is a land where dreams can come true and wishes can be fulfilled. We all know that, but sometimes we forget.

I believe that anyone with drive and vision—*anyone*—can achieve success in this country. Here, being born into poverty does not mean you are condemned to spend the rest of your life in poverty. Being born to parents who had little education does not mean that you, too, are condemned to grow up uneducated. Being the child of a father who works in a coal mine or a single mother who works on an assembly line or at a grocery store checkout counter does not mean you will need to settle for the same choices.

Sometimes we forget that this is not true for people in most of the rest of the world.

I think my own story proves the point. By almost any measure, I have been incredibly successful, yet it's been anything but a smooth journey. My early successes from selling newspapers to paving driveways to starting my own heating and air conditioning business, grossing a million dollars at the age of twenty, all led me to selling franchises, creating the Small Business Center, starting Franchise America, and then taking a partner into that company. The Food Saver earned me a place in the history books while becoming my first major product infomercial, a runaway success that gave me the courage for everything that followed.

When I walked away from the Franchise America partnership, I left almost empty-handed, except for the self-confidence in my ability to start all over. Under the umbrella of a new company, Quantum, I discovered Arnold Morris, hitting the airwaves with the infomercial selling the knives, followed by the Daily Mixer and the Great Wok of China. Those products plus the timely decision to go international, catapulted us in eighteen months from zero to $140 million in annual sales.

And then it all crashed in that Chapter 11 bankruptcy.

Once again I managed, as they say, to snatch victory from the jaws of defeat, becoming a partner in National Media and helping to take the company from $100 million to $500 million a year and the stock from $1.50 to over $20 per share.

After three years, I was ready to move on again, to run my

own operation, this time landing on my feet creating an infomercial arm, HSN Direct, for the Home Shopping Network.

When Home Shopping was sold and came under the management of Barry Diller, the esteemed former CEO of Paramount Pictures, he turned out to have a dislike for the infomercial business. Clearly it was time to end my HSN partnership. For the fourth time in my career, I needed to define a new path for myself. In 1998, still with Tim at my side as always, I started a new infomercial company named Reliant, which has since morphed into OmniReliant. As I write this, the company has recently raised $17 million and purchased the production studio where many of our infomercials have been shot over the past fourteen years.

It has been a career of successes, setbacks, and new beginnings. I have come to believe that for every entrepreneur and businessperson in this land of opportunity, few setbacks will ever be so overwhelming that they cannot be seen as the opening of a door to a new opportunity.

I believe my career to date can stand as testimony to that favorite line of mine quoted at the beginning of this book: "Whatever you vividly imagine, ardently desire, sincerely believe, and enthusiastically act upon must inevitably come to pass."

INDEX

"visco-elastic memory foam,"
188–189

W

Wally Woks. *See also*
  Great Wok of China
  copyright infringement, 93–94
  infomercials, 70–76, 92–94
  sale under a different name,
    92–93
Warden Bob, 213
Warner Amex Cable, 39
Warwick Hotel, 70
Westinghouse Credit, 19–20
Westminster Company, 73
WH Smith company, 102–103,
    113, 201
White, Ben, 137

White, Vanna, 88, 212
Williams Sonoma, 36
Wolfman Jack
  free tickets, 215
  live studio audience,
    214–216
  music infomercial,
    first-ever, 217
  risk taking, 217
  rock-and-roll favorites, 216
  sock hop infomercial, 215
Wolk, Beryl, 47–48, 54, 56, 69

Y

Yellow Pages, 20
Young Entrepreneurs Organization
    (YEO), 30, 69, 86
YTB Travel, 208

ABOUT THE AUTHOR

Kevin Harrington was born in Cincinnati to a mother who shaped his values and a father who, as owner of a series of restaurants, pubs, and nightclubs, set an example of long hours and dedication to work. Kevin started earning pocket money at age nine. Before he was old enough to drive, Kevin and a friend launched a driveway resurfacing business that some weeks brought in as much as $3,000 profit; as a sixteenth birthday present, Kevin bought himself a new MG sports car—for cash.

By the time he entered college, Kevin was running his own heating/air-conditioning business, grossing $1 million a year. Seeking wider horizons, he created a business brokering company, putting would-be businesspeople and investors together with franchise owners and those with a local store or company to sell. He soon turned to television as a way of reaching wider audiences for these messages.

This use of television led him to the idea of selling not just businesses, but products as well, and he was soon purchasing unused overnight airtime from the Discovery Channel and other national cable TV outlets. He was pioneering the half-hour product show—the infomercial—as what seemed like nothing more than the next logical step. Today the infomercial is, of course, a billion-dollar global sales tool.

The most dramatic step in establishing the infomercial came when Kevin paid one of his frequent visits to a home-product show and discovered an amazing pitchman selling kitchen knives; the pitchman was Arnold Morris, and the product was what we now know as Ginsu knives. Since then, Kevin has produced hundreds of infomercials, and these shows have made more than a hundred people into millionaires and multi-millionaires.

Kevin cofounded the Cincinnati charitable organization called Fun Raisers, the Electronic Retailing Association, and the international group now known as the Entrepreneurs Organization. He lives in St. Petersburg, Florida.